An
INTENTIONAL
Walk WITH
GOD

A 101-Days Journey

Dr. Yvonne L. Terrell-Powell
and Jenel A. Terrell-Matias

xulon PRESS

Copyright © 2018 by Dr. Yvonne L. Terrell-Powell and Jenel A.Terrell-Matias

An Intentional Walk with God: A 101-Days Journey
by Dr. Yvonne L. Terrell-Powell and Jenel A.Terrell-Matias

Printed in the United States of America.

ISBN 9781498499552

All rights reserved solely by the author. The author guarantees all contents are orig-
inal and do not infringe upon the legal rights of any other person or work. No part of
this book may be reproduced in any form without the permission of the author. The
views expressed in this book are not necessarily those of the publisher.

Unless otherwise indicated, Scripture quotations taken from the King James Version
(KJV) – public domain

www.xulonpress.com

ACKNOWLEDGEMENTS

Special Thanks to: Duvalle Daniel, Jewel Fink, Amesha Matias, Gerreid Matias, Mishael Powell, Uriah Powell, Speak Life Ministries Women's Group, SmoothWriting, Alyce Taylor, Thomazine Vaughn, and Joanne Warner

We want to thank our parents Spess W. Terrell and Jean S. Terrell who we love dearly. We also want to thank our phenomenal Nana who most recently passed away at 102 years old.

♥

*And Jesus said, "It is the spirit the quickeneth; the flesh profiteth nothing: the words that **I speak** unto you, they are spirit, and they are **life"**
(Jn. 6:63).*

♥

CONTENTS

FORWARD

Jenel and Yvonne began writing and spreading the Good News of Jesus Christ long before deciding to write this book. They love God and remain committed to doing His will. They intentionally sought to have an intimate relationship with God and have been blessed by His love. God gave Jenel the gift of motivating others through writing and speaking, and He gave Yvonne the gift of motivating others through speaking and teaching, or at least that's what they believe. A few years ago, God opened up new gifts for them. He opened up the gift of teaching the Word of God for Jenel. He opened up the gift of writing His message for Yvonne. While He spoke to them at different times and in different ways, one consistent message was that they needed to be more intentional with their relationship with Him. He called them to ministry. Yvonne and Jenel are not "church ministers." They are women of God with a ministry birthed by God. They are women of God with a message from God; a message that has been created out of God's love for everyone— a message of faith, hope, and love.

This book was inspired by the Holy Spirit and written out of their obedience to and love for God. It consists of personal stories, poems and messages that speak about love, courage, faith, trust, hope, joy, and commitment. It is not just a daily journal or devotional. It is a personal diary that allows you to share the secrets of your heart, the fears of life, the victories of your day, and the love that flows from your soul.

There is a message from God wrapped up in each page of this book. The key message is that God loves you. He wants to hear from you. He desires to have a closer and more intimate relationship with you. He wants to guide you in His perfect way. God wants you to open up your heart to trust that He will create new opportunities, insights, and renew your heart and spirit. God is faithful, and His unconditional love for you is steadfast and everlasting.

AN INTENTIONAL WALK
WITH GOD – GUIDE

We pray you find this guide a helpful tool as you take your daily walk with God. An Intentional Walk with God urges you to draw closer to your heavenly Father by daily seeking God for a 101-day period. Each day's walk begins with the reading of a scripture, followed by the authors' interpretation of the verse or verses through personal stories, poems, observations and insights that illuminate the power of God's Word.

Begin each day with God by reading one of the messages from this book. You can start with any message you want, just pick a new one each day for 101 days. At the end of each message, you'll find a faith affirmation, a prayer, and a space to write a "Dear God" letter. Once you have read the message, prayer, and faith affirmation, write down the faith affirmation and recite it throughout your day.

It will be important for you to focus on having a positive attitude, an attitude of victory. Your strength and power comes from God so plan to have a victorious day. Think on those thoughts that are right, good, and positive (Phil. 4:8). Praise God. With praise and a heart of thanksgiving, your spirit is rejuvenated every second, minute, and hour.

If your day seems to be getting the best of you, talk to God about what is going on and how you feel. Remember God is with you, and He loves you. He goes before you to make the crooked places straight and the rough patches smooth (Isa. 45:2). Ask Him to help you get through your day and trust that He will. Then once again praise and thank Him.

At the end of the day, put your heart before the Lord and talk to Him about your day. Give thanks to the Lord, for the many blessings He has granted to you (1 Thess. 5:18). Allow your thoughts and emotions to flow. Write your "Dear God" letter, which can include words of thanksgiving, adoration, confessions, and dedication. You can include what you have taken from the message of the day, or you can share any part of your journey with God. You may also choose to draw a picture or write a poem or a message you received from

God. It's your message and letter so do whatever feels right for you. Close your day knowing that God goes beyond the end of your day because there is no end to God, and He is working everything out for your good (Rom. 8:28). You can rest knowing that God loves you. Oh, how He loves you.

As you walk with God on this journey....

1. Open your day with praise and worship. God loves to hear from you. (Ps. 95, 96, 105, 150).

2. Put your heart before God (Prov. 4:23; Mk. 12:30; 2 Thess. 3:5) and listen for His voice (Ps. 29).

3. Ask God to reveal the areas in your life that need healing and growth (Ps. 139:23-24) and to give you wisdom and understanding (Prov. 4:7).

4. Ask God to show you how to do things that are different from your usual pattern or schedule. Changing what is routine allows God more room to create His routine.

5. Read and listen to the Word of God and listen to praise and worship music.

6. Memorize and meditate on scriptures that support your area of healing and growth (Ps. 1:1-2, 19:14).

7. Talk with individuals who will support you on this journey. You may choose to have an accountability partner.

8. Speak Life. Speak words of love, faith, hope, encouragement, peace, and power.

9. Keep track of your days and progress and keep walking on this life changing journey with God.

10. Close your day with praise, worship, thanksgiving, and a prayer to God.

Come and walk with God on this life changing journey. You will be blessed "exceeding abundantly above all that you can ask or think according to [His] power that works in you" (Eph. 3:20).

A 101-Days Journey –
Covenant Letter

So teach us to number our days, that we may apply our hearts unto wisdom (Ps. 90:12).

Dear God,

I, _____, commit to a 101-Days Intentional Walk with You. I desire to have an intimate relationship with You. Your Word says, ". . . for he that cometh to God must believe that He is, and that He is a rewarder of them that diligently seek Him" (Heb. 11:6). I have prayerfully sought You on my intentions to commit to walking daily with You. I believe that You will meet me where I am and walk with me. I have had some good and bad days, but I believe that my best days are yet to come. You are the hope of my life and my salvation.

I believe that this walk will be life changing for me and my life will never be the same. I expect that this walk will draw me closer to You. I will spend more time talking with You, listening to You, and resting and abiding in You – in Your unconditional love. I will enter into the oneness that You have created for our relationship. I will enter into Your loving presence where You will minister to my heart and spirit, and I will become more like You: full of glory, peace, love, and righteousness.

Father, I thank You for Your love, mercy, joy, and grace. I thank You for opening my heart to receive You. I thank You for walking with me and guiding me into Your perfect way. I thank You for today. Most of all, I thank You for loving me. I love You, too.

Love,

Date:
Day #:

LORD TODAY

Take therefore no thought for the morrow: for the morrow shall take thought for the things of itself. Sufficient unto the day is the evil thereof (Matt. 6:34).

I sat and talked with a close friend. We talked about the love, power, and greatness of God. We talked about needing God each and every day. He talked about his mother and how she often said "Lord Today." She called on the Lord and lavished Him with praise and thanksgiving. When her heart was heavy, she called on Him for assurance that He would make a way. Other days she called on God to ask Him to protect her children and to keep them safe. Sometimes she just called out "Lord Today" and allowed God to speak to her heart. She called on Him believing that He loved her and would answer her call.

We also talked about how we often cry out "Lord Today." With each breath, we acknowledge the power, love, and grace of God. With each call, we place our trust and faith in God. Our heartfelt calls acknowledge that God is sovereign and has control of our today. We trust that God loves us and will make provisions for us (Matt. 6:33). He is the only answer to our today. Won't you take time to call on the Lord today? He will make a difference in your today.

Lord today,
I praise Your holy name.
I acknowledge that You are my Father and have been more than good to me.
I ask You to speak to my heart and guide me to Your perfect peace (Isa. 26:3).
I declare "How excellent is [Your] name in all the earth!" (Ps. 8:1).

Lord today,
Hear my cry; I need You.
Shield me with Your love and favor.
Renew a right spirit in me (Ps. 51:10);

1

Restore my soul, and
Do exceeding abundantly above all that I can ask or think (Eph. 3:20).

Lord today,
I will keep my heart and mind focused on You.
I will not worry about tomorrow (Matt. 6:34).
I will trust that if Your eye is on the sparrow, surely You are watching over me.
I will bless You with my whole heart (Ps. 9:1)!
Lord today, I love You always and forever!

Faith Affirmation: *Lord today. . . . .*

Prayer: Lord, I thank You for today (Ps. 118:24). I thank You for another opportunity to declare, "How excellent is [Your] name in all the earth!" (Ps. 8:1). I thank You for being Lord of my life. I thank You for loving me. No matter my circumstances or feelings, I know that I need You today and for evermore.

Dear God Letter: Talk to God about your **Today**. Ask Him to give you insight into your **Today**.

Dear God,

THE LORD IS MY SHEPHERD

The LORD is my shepherd; I shall not want . . . (Ps. 23:1).

D avid was a shepherd boy who was called by God and anointed King of Israel. As a shepherd, he was responsible for his father's sheep. He had to spend time with them so that they would trust him and answer only to his voice. The sheep needed not to fear for their shepherd was their guide, caretaker, and protector. David provided for their needs and knew all about them. He knew that if he left the sheep to their own care and devices, they would be harmed, devoured, or even taken. Without his care and guidance, the sheep would go astray and become prey for wild animals and other predators, and be vulnerable to natural conditions – storms, floods, ravines. David was the master of the sheep, and as their master, he would protect them even if it threatened his life.

In Psalm 23, David establishes God as the shepherd and identifies himself as one of His sheep. He writes "The Lord is my shepherd." The Lord, I AM THAT I AM, Jehovah, Elohim (the Creator of the heavens and earth), was his shepherd. His shepherd loved him. He needed not to fear or want because God was his ultimate protector, provider, and guide. God, the Creator of the heavens and earth and all that is within it (Ps. 24:1), knew exactly what he needed to live a healthy and anointed life, and "Though [he] walked through the valley of the shadow of death, [he would] fear no evil for [God was] with him…" (Ps. 23:4). As his shepherd, God would always be right there no matter the circumstances or situation. He trusted the Lord, I AM THAT I AM (Ex. 3:14), the One that was always more than he needed him to be.

The Lord is also your shepherd, and you are one of His sheep. In the book of John, Jesus states, "I am the good shepherd: the good shepherd giveth his life for the sheep . . . and [I] know my sheep and am known of mine. . . I lay down my life for the sheep" (Jn. 10:11, 14-15). The Lord loves you so much that He sent His son, Jesus Christ, to save the world— to

3

save you. Let the Lord, be your shepherd and lead you down the path of righteousness and restore your soul (Ps. 23:3) with joy, laughter, hope, peace, health, and prosperity. Won't you let the Good Shepherd guide you today and for evermore?

Psalm 23

> (1)The Lord is my shepherd; I shall not want. (2) He maketh me to lie down in green pastures: He leadeth me beside the still waters. (3) He restoreth my soul: He leadeth me in the paths of righteousness for His name's sake. (4) Yea, though I walk through the valley of the shadow of death, I will fear no evil: for thou art with me; thy rod and thy staff they comfort me. (5) Thou preparest a table before me in the presence of mine enemies: thou anointest my head with oil; my cup runneth over. (6) Surely goodness and mercy shall follow me all the days of my life: and I will dwell in the house of the Lord forever.

Faith Affirmation: *The Lord is my Shepherd and I trust Him.*

Prayer: Father, I thank You for today (Ps. 118:24), another day to be in a relationship with You. How wonderful and "excellent is [Your] name in all the earth" (Ps. 8:1). You are my Shepherd (Ps. 23:1), and I am safe with You.

Dear God Letter: Talk to God about your day. The **Lord is your Shepherd.**

Dear God,

Date:
Day #:

WHAT WOULD IT HURT?

But ye have an unction (anointing) *from the Holy One, and ye know all things (1 Jn. 2:20).*

What **would it hurt?** First John 2:20 states, "But [you] have an unction (anointing) from the Holy One, and [you] know all things." If you know all things because of the Holy Spirit, why don't you acknowledge the Holy Spirit when you are given a directive, answer, or instructions from Him? When it came to my hearing the Holy Spirit and then my response to Him, I thought I was doing pretty well. NOT! I soon found out that in certain areas I was doing well but not in others. I needed to change my response to the Father.

My relationship with the Father is first and foremost in my life. The Father loves me, and I love Him. He has given you and me a purpose and an expected end (Jer. 29:11). To reach our expected end, we must daily allow ourselves to be led by the Holy Spirit and to experience God's anointing.

In acknowledging my desire to be led by the Holy Spirit, He began to show me the areas that needed improvement in my life. The Holy Spirit showed me that I did not trust His judgment when it came to Him taking

What would it hurt?

care of my needs. I asked God to clearly show me the times I did not adhere to His voice. Here are just a few: The Holy Spirit said to me "Put your hat in your purse." The request sounded simple to my spirit, but I (my flesh) did not see a rain cloud in the sky. Can you guess what happened? It rained 2 inches on that day. The Holy Spirit told me to put my glasses in my purse. I (my flesh) said that I didn't need my glasses because I would be home before dark. Guess again; it was overcast by late afternoon. These two incidences were far apart, and thus they did not seem so important. Then, a third incident occurred, and I realized that I was being disobedient to the voice of my Father.

On the third incident, the Holy Spirit requested that I get some gas before traveling to my next destination. Of course, I did not take the time to stop at the gas station, which left me driving on fumes and praying that I wouldn't run out of gas on the freeway. You can laugh now because it is funny, and I'm quite sure you have had a similar experience, an experience that caused you discomfort or placed you in an awkward situation because you did not follow the direction of the Holy Spirit.

After this third experience, I heard the Holy Spirit say, **"What would it hurt?"** What would it hurt, if you did as I asked you to do? **What would it hurt** you to be moved by the unction (anointing) of the Holy One? Stop allowing your flesh to question my thoughts. My thoughts are good and will give you an expected end. "For my thoughts are not your thoughts. Neither are your ways my ways" (Isa. 55:8). If you would have put the hat in your purse, your hair would not have gotten wet. If you would have put your glasses in your purse, you would not have had to strain your eyes and drive in the dark. If you would have gotten gas when I requested you to, you would not have been driving on fumes, praying for the next gas station. I, the Holy Spirit, the One who has already gone where you will be going, knew that the gas station that you decided to stop at right off the freeway was closed. You don't need to know what I know. You need to do what I ask of you.

How many "what would it hurt" moments do you have in an hour, a day, a week, or month? Be honest with yourself. The flesh is never willing, and it is an excellent excuse maker. The Holy Spirit is always willing and always patient. The Word is clear that we have an "unction from the Holy One to know all things" (1 Jn. 2:20). God's Word is fresh and new every morning. At the sound of His voice, His sheep (you and me) follow Him (Jn. 10:4). We know that God has gone before us and made the crooked places straight (Isa. 45:2), which allows us to walk in His anointing every day. God loves you and has only made plans that will benefit your expected end and His kingdom (Jer. 29:11).

I believe that because of God's anointing, we are more than capable of doing all that He has called and chosen us to do. We must be obedient to God's direction. **What would it hurt?** The only thing that it will hurt will be Satan's [schemes] and plans to destroy our divine purpose and calling — Praise God. Take the time to follow the Word and voice of the Holy Spirit. You will be blessed. **What would it hurt?**

Faith Affirmation: *I will acknowledge the voice of the Lord. What would it hurt?*

Prayer: Father, this is the day that You have made for me (Ps. 118:24). I will bless Your name forever (Ps. 115:18). You dwell in me (1 Cor. 3:16) and have given me the unction (anointing) to know all things (1 Jn. 2:20). I will listen and obey Your voice. It is Your voice that guides me (Jn. 10:4) and will lead me to my expected end (Jer. 29:11).

Dear God Letter: Talk to God about your day. You have the unction from the Holy Spirit to do the will of the Father. **What would it hurt?**

Dear God,

Date:

Day #:

ATTITUDE ADJUSTMENT

For as he thinketh in his heart, so is he. . . (Prov. 23:7).

I remember a time that I lost weight; well at least I thought I had lost weight. My clothes were fitting looser, and I just knew that I had lost at least 8 or 10 pounds. I walked around thinking I was all that; Miss Good-lookin of the Year. With my new weight loss and positive image, I pranced around in my husband's face just looking for those compliments and marriage perks. Oh, I was looking good and feeling great. I exuded a spirit of confidence, happiness, and sexiness. Yes, sexiness.

Several months later, I visited my physician. I usually balk at having to get on the scale. This time I just stepped on the scale with confidence. I didn't even look at the weight that was being recorded by the nurse. I didn't need to look because I was looking and feeling great.

When I met with the physician, she reviewed my medical chart and reported her findings. She told me that I had lost one pound since my last visit with her. I said, "How many?" She said "one pound." I was shocked. I started giggling right at that moment. I had lost only one pound, not the 8 – 10 that I was expecting. When I left my appointment, I immediately called my sister and told her the news. We just busted up laughing. I laughed so hard that I started to cry. You're probably cracking up right now, because I'm laughing while I am writing this story. Oh, to delight in our experiences in life.

At some unknown point in time, my attitude had adjusted about my weight, appearance, and personal perspective. I saw a slimmer person and felt more confident. My view of myself had changed and positively impacted my day-to-day experiences. I had an attitude adjustment because of something that I perceived and believed. I stopped laughing about my situation, and I challenged myself to continue to see myself as confident, beautiful and sexy. I determined in my heart and mind that I would not go back to my old attitude. This experience showed me that my thoughts can change my attitude, and your thoughts can change yours, too.

Upon accepting Christ into our lives, God asks us to see ourselves as He sees us. We are fearfully and wonderfully made (Ps. 139:14). We are created in God's image and likeness (Gen. 1:26) and filled with God Himself, the Holy Spirit (1 Cor. 3:16). We can overcome anything in the name of Jesus. "We are more than conquerors through Him (Jesus Christ) that loved us" (Rom. 8:37). We may make mistakes, but mistakes are not us; they are just mistakes. We may have negative thoughts, but the negative thoughts are not us; they are just thoughts. We may be diagnosed with cancer, leukemia, HIV/AIDS; that's not us; it's just a diagnosis. We are the temple of the Most High God (1 Cor. 3:16).

My thoughts can change my attitude.

Take the opportunity to adjust your attitude and see yourself healed, free, strong, courageous, special, loving, and the gorgeous person God has called you to be. I was all that before the physician told me I had only lost "one pound" and all that afterwards, because I challenged myself to see the gorgeousness in me in the name of Jesus. Do you need an attitude adjustment? If so, call on the name of Jesus and begin to see yourself through the eyes and heart of your Creator? There is a saying, "Free your mind and the rest will follow."

Faith Affirmation: *I see myself as God sees me.*

Prayer: Father, I thank You for this day (Ps. 118:4). You are great. "I will praise [You] with my whole heart" (Ps. 138:1). I thank You for creating me in Your image and likeness (Gen. 1:26) and filling me with You, the Holy Spirit (1 Cor. 3:16). Lord, help me to see myself as You see me. I am Your child, and I am fearfully and wonderfully made (Ps. 139:14).

Dear God Letter: Talk to God about your day. Remember to make **attitude adjustments** daily. You are the temple of the Holy Spirit.

Dear God,

ARE YOU ANOINTED TO SING UNTO THE LORD?

And when he had consulted with the people, he appointed singers unto the Lord, and that should praise the beauty of holiness, as they went out before the army, and to say, Praise the LORD; for his mercy endureth forever (2 Chron. 20:21).

Jehoshaphat, the king of Judah, was a righteous man of God and lived by God's commandments (2 Chron. 17:2-5). Yet, Jehoshaphat still faced adversity in his life. The children of Moab, Ammon and Mount Seir, who were enemies of Israel, joined together to invade King Jehoshaphat and the people of Judah. King Jehoshaphat knew that his army was no match for the invading armies and proclaimed a fast throughout Judah (2 Chron. 20:3). He also brought the people of Judah and Jerusalem together to pray and ask God to help them (2 Chron. 20:4-12).

God heard the prayers of his people and answered saying, "Be not afraid nor dismayed by reason of this great multitude; for the battle is not yours but God's (2 Chron. 20:15). . . Ye shall not need to fight in this battle: set yourselves, stand ye still, and see the salvation of the Lord with you, O Judah and Jerusalem: fear not, nor be dismayed; tomorrow go out against them: for the Lord will be with you" (2 Chron. 20:17).

As the people of Judah and Jerusalem went out before the Moabites, Ammonites, and Mount Seir armies, Jehoshaphat reminded them to believe in the Lord their God (2 Chron. 20:20). Then as directed by God, Jehoshaphat appointed singers unto the Lord. The singers would praise God and the beauty of His holiness, as they went out before the armies. The singers were instructed to say, **"Praise the Lord; for His mercy endureth forever"** (2 Chron. 20:21). For Judah and Jerusalem to win this battle, they needed to praise the Lord and believe that the Lord would establish them and allow them to prosper (2 Chron. 2:20). When the people began to sing

13

and to praise the Lord, God set ambushments against their enemies, and their enemies destroyed each other (2 Chron. 20:22-23).

After their enemies destroyed each other, Jehoshaphat and his people found more riches and precious jewels than they could carry away. In fact, it took them three days to gather all the riches and jewels. Then they assembled themselves in a place, the valley of Berachah and blessed the Lord (2 Chron. 2:25-26). They weren't tired from fighting because God had fought their battle. Their hearts were filled with joy; "for the Lord had made them to rejoice over their enemies" (2 Chron. 20:27). The people of Judah and Jerusalem entered the house of the Lord playing stringed instruments and harps and trumpets (2 Chron. 20:28). I can imagine they praised the beauty of holiness and said, **"Praise the Lord, for His mercy endureth forever"** (2 Chron. 20:21). "And the fear of God was on all kingdoms of those countries, when they had heard that the Lord fought against the enemies of Israel. So the realm of Jehoshaphat was quiet: for his God gave him rest round about" (2 Chron. 20:29-30).

Often we forget to stand still and see the salvation of the Lord (2 Chron. 20:17). We fight a battle when God requested that we stand still and sing; **Praise the Lord, for His mercy; His lovingkindness endures forever**. We forget because we have not accepted our appointment to sing. We have not accepted our appointment because we choose to stay in a state of mind that says, "I need to fight this battle; thus singing won't work; just praising won't help, and if I dare stand still, I will lose." Everyone at the battle was not told to sing, but they were all told to stand still and see the salvation of the Lord. When you are appointed to a position, you must know that through Christ you are more than capable of fulfilling your position.

Your appointment as a praise singer for the Lord takes mind shifting and faith. As you know, your mind can empower, encourage, and enable you. It can also hinder, condemn, and discourage you. If you believe you are an appointed singer and you respond as an appointed singer, then you are. The position does not require much. It only requires that you believe and **Praise the Lord for His mercy endures forever** (2 Chron. 20:21). The reality is this; praising the beauty of holiness tears down walls, destroys yokes and strongholds, binds and loosens, creates, restores, causes ambushments, confuses the enemy, keeps you joyous and peaceful, keeps your heart and mind focused on God and most importantly, defeats the enemy. No matter the circumstances and no matter how big the enemy may appear to be, you must praise the beauty of holiness as you face your circumstance. At the end of the battle, you will receive a blessing from the Lord that will be more than you can imagine.

14

Faith Affirmation: *I will praise the Lord, for His mercy endures forever.*

Prayer: Lord, I thank You for all that You have done for me today (Ps. 118:24; 1 Thess. 5:18). "No weapon that is formed against [me] shall prosper; and every tongue that shall rise against [me] in judgment thou shalt condemn. This is the heritage of the servants of the Lord, and [our] righteousness is of [You]" (Isa. 54:17). I will set myself and stand still in Your anointing. I will praise the beauty of Your holiness and say, **"Praise the Lord, Your mercy endureth forever!"** (2 Chron. 20:21).

Dear God Letter: Talk to God about your day. **You are appointed to sing unto the Lord,** "Praise the Lord, for His mercy endureth forever."

Dear God,

GET UNDERSTANDING

Wisdom is the principal thing; therefore get wisdom: and with all thy getting get understanding (Prov. 4:7).

Whatever the season of your life, it is imperative that you understand who you are in Christ and what direction God is taking you. You will receive this understanding by seeking God. As you seek Him, He will speak to you and reveal His Word in a very clear way. With clarity, you will be able to follow God's instructions for your life. You will hear His voice, know His voice, and understand His instructions (Jn. 10:27). Your vision will not tarry (Hab. 2:3). You will fulfill your purpose in the name of Jesus.

God requests that you get into your purposed position in Christ. You are able to get into your position through your relationship with the Father and the Son. God loves you and sent His Son so that you would be reconciled to Him. He also sent the Holy Spirit to comfort, guide, and reveal His Word. God loves you and desires that you would enter into a loving, trusting relationship with Him. The Father knows that His wisdom and understanding will guide you into His loving arms, where you will find His love, joy, peace, and favor, where you will find life. Without His wisdom and under-standing, you are lost. You are more susceptible to being bothered, battered, and beaten by the weapons of Satan. However, with insight from the Holy Spirit, and your desire to do His will, His Word reveals a clearer path to your divine destiny.

Get into your purposed position in Christ.

God is always with you and desires to have an intimate relationship with you. Out of His love for you, He desires that you, in turn, love Him. Our Father requests that you spend time with Him and experience His love, peace, joy, wisdom, and understanding. "[He loves] them that love [Him]; and those that seek Him early [or diligently] shall find [Him]" (Prov.

8:17). God knows you. Do you know Him? Do you know the sound of His voice? If you have an ear to hear and a heart for Christ, you will receive His wisdom and understanding. "Understanding is a wellspring of life unto [those] that [have] it; but the instruction of fools is folly" (Prov. 16:22).

Faith Affirmation: *I will obtain wisdom and understanding from the Lord.*

Prayer: Father, I thank You for this day (Ps. 118:24). You are "righteous in all of [Your] ways, and holy in all [Your] works" (Ps. 145:17). "The fear of [You] is the beginning of wisdom: and the knowledge of the Holy is understanding" (Prov. 9:10). I have peace knowing that Your wisdom and understanding shall guide me always and forever.

Dear God Letter: Talk to God about your day. Seek God for more wisdom and **get understanding** about your purpose and direction from the Father in the name of Jesus.

Dear God,

Date:
Day #:

THE LORD'S PURPOSE

There are many [plans] in a man's heart; nevertheless the counsel of the Lord, that shall stand (Prov. 19:21).

It is important that you understand that God created you intentionally for His purpose. He did not create one mistake. As He was creating you, God the Father, God the Son, and God the Holy Spirit, "saved [you], and called [you] with a holy calling, not according to [your] works, but according to His own purpose and grace, which was given [to you] in Christ Jesus before the world began" (2 Tim. 1:9). God predetermined your existence. He created, sanctified (Jer. 1:5), and called you to complete His divine purpose for your life. God loves you, and He has given you the Holy Spirit to provide you with the guidance and teaching needed to fulfill your divine purpose.

You are required to accomplish God's purpose in your life, and you will, but will it take longer than God intended? When you don't spend time with Him, you lack the much needed wisdom for your day. On the other hand, when you spend time in God's Word, God the Holy Spirit has something to bring to your remembrance for your day— some rich wisdom and understanding. "Let the word of Christ dwell in you richly in all wisdom. . ." (Col. 3:16). With wisdom, you will adjust your plans to line up with God's counsel.

Do you believe your life is going the way that God intended, purposed and predetermined it to go? If you're not sure, seek God. Jesus is the "author and finisher of [your] faith who for the joy that was set before Him endured the cross . . . and is set down at the right hand of the throne God" (Heb. 12:2). Put your heart before the Lord, and He will direct your path (Prov. 3:5-6).

Faith Affirmation: *I will allow God's purpose to prevail in my life.*

Prayer: Father, I thank You for providing me with another day (Ps. 118:24) to strive to do Your will. From the depths of my heart, I praise Your holy name (Ps. 29:2). It is my desire to accept Your counsel and allow it to guide and direct my life. I place my heart before You and ask that You search my heart, and if there be anything that is not pleasing to You, show me how to change it (Ps. 139:23-24).

Dear God Letter: Talk to God about your day. With wisdom you will understand **the Lord's Purpose** for your life.

Dear God,

RELEASE GOD AND HE WILL DO THE REST

Quench not the [Holy] Spirit (1 Thess. 5:19).

The men of the armies of the living God were well prepared to fight men of their size and stature; not Goliath the Philistine giant. His appearance, voice, and excellent battle record put fear in their hearts. None of the men believed that they could defeat this giant. He would destroy them. Along came a young anointed shepherd boy, David, who had been asked by his father to go to the battlefield and check on his brothers. He had killed a bear and a lion by the mighty hand of God (1 Sam. 17:34-35), but he had not fought on the battlefield, nor had he fought with a giant. Yet, David knew that God was all-powerful and almighty. He need not fear this giant. As he saw the men scurrying and heard the threats of Goliath, he asked, "For who is this uncircumcised Philistine, that he should [challenge] the armies of the living God?" (1 Sam. 17:26). David knew that whoever he was, he would not be around for long. This Philistine was coming down by the mighty hand of God, "for the battle [was] the Lords" (1 Sam. 17:47).

To fight Goliath, David chose the weapons that God had blessed. He chose his staff, which had been used to lead, guide, and protect him and the sheep. Out of the brook, he chose five smooth stones. These stones would be used in his sling to defeat Goliath. Once he selected the fifth stone, he was ready to do battle with Goliath, and he headed in the direction of the Philistine (1 Sam. 17:40). David had five opportunities to take down Goliath with one of the stones. He loaded his sling with one of the stones and released it, and at the same time He released God to do His will. The stone hit Goliath and "sunk into his forehead; and [Goliath] fell upon his

> *God is all-powerful and almighty.*

21

face to the earth . . . David ran, and stood upon [Goliath] . . . and cut off his head" (1 Sam. 17:49-51).

What has God given to you to take down and destroy the Goliath who manifests as depression, disappointment, low self-esteem, despair, loneliness, rejection, lack of forgiveness, addiction, and fear? He has given you Him, the Lord strong, powerful, and mighty. He has given you a wide range of gifts, skills, and talents. He has also given you the whole armor of God.

Paul, an apostle of Christ Jesus wrote,

> "Put on the whole armor of God, that ye may be able to stand against the [schemes] of the devil. . . Wherefore take unto you the whole armor of God, that ye may be able to withstand in the evil day, and having done all, to stand. Stand therefore, having your loins girt about with truth, and having on the breastplate of righteousness; and your feet shod with the preparation of the gospel of peace; above all, taking the shield of faith, wherewith ye shall be able to quench all the fiery darts of the wicked. And take the helmet of salvation, and the sword of the Spirit, which is the word of God: Praying always with all prayer and supplication in the Spirit, and watching thereunto with all perseverance and supplication for all saints . . ." (Eph. 6:11 – 18).

Release God into your life situation by trusting and loving Him. Release God to fight your battle. He is strong and mighty in battle (Ps. 24:8).

Faith Affirmation: *I will release the Holy Spirit in my life.*

Prayer: Lord, I thank You for another day to stand strong in You and rejoice (Ps. 118:24). You alone are worthy to be praised forever and ever (Ps. 96:4). You are my protector and a strong tower. It is my desire to decrease and to release You to do Your will in my life. I have committed to keeping on Your armor (Eph. 6:13-14). It is comforting to know that You love me and will fight my battles (1 Sam. 17:47).

Dear God Letter: Talk to God about your day. Remember to **release God and He will do the rest** for you.

Dear God,

Date:
Day #:

UTMOST CONFIDENCE

*My soul, wait thou only upon God; for my expectation is from Him . . .
In God is my salvation and my glory: the rock of my strength, and my
refuge, is in God (Ps. 62:5, 7).*

Father, I have utmost confidence in You.

*A*s *Your child,*
I am confident that You love me (Jer. 31:3).
I am confident that nothing shall separate me from Your love which is in
Christ Jesus [my] Lord (Rom. 8:38-39).
I am confident that You live within me, and You are directing me to my
expected end.
I am certain that You will never leave nor forsake me (Heb. 13:5).

With each day,
I am confident that You have pulled me from my defeat of yesterday into
a new day of joy, peace, and victory (Ps. 30:5).
I am positive that You will make an ordinary day into an extraordinary day.
I am convinced that You will intervene as I move with faith (Heb. 11).
I am confident that through You I am more than a conqueror (Rom. 8:37).

As I walk on this journey,
I declare as the Hebrew boys declared that You will deliver me in Your way
and in Your time (Dan. 3).
I confess as David confessed that You will deliver me from my enemies
(Ps.18:3).
I believe as Hannah believed that You will answer my prayers (1 Sam. 1).
I believe as the multitudes of people believed that You will perform mir-
acles (Jn. 6:2).
I proclaim that You are my Lord and Savior.

25

As I move and breathe,
I am certain that You are my strength and my shield (Ps. 28:7).
I am confident that You will teach me Your way and lead me in a plain path (Ps. 27:11).
I am confident that You will protect me like a shield and surround me with Your favor (Ps. 5:12).
I am confident that You will inhabit my praises (Ps. 22:3) and bless me.

As I seek You,
I am confident that I was created to praise You, and
I will praise You with all my heart and soul.
I will magnify and exalt Your holy name.
I will embrace Your love and thank You for Your gift of salvation (Eph. 2:8-9).
I will wait with confidence and expectation knowing that You will answer my prayers exceeding abundantly above all that I can or think (Eph. 3:20).
Lord, I love You, and I have the utmost confidence in You!

Faith Affirmation: *I have the utmost confidence in God.*

Prayer: Father, I thank You for this day (Ps. 118:24) and all that You have done for me (1 Thess. 5:18). You are "great and greatly to be praised" (Ps. 96:4). "My heart trusted in [You]. . . (Ps. 28:7) and . . . my soul, wait thou only upon [You]; for my expectation is from [You]" (Ps. 62:5). My hope is in You, and I have the utmost confidence in You.

Dear God Letter: Talk to God about your day. When you trust God, you will have the **utmost confidence** that He will do the impossible.

Dear God,

Date:
Day #:

IS GOD'S GRACE SUFFICIENT?

*And [God] said unto me, My grace is sufficient for thee: for my strength
is made perfect in weakness. . . (2 Cor. 12:9).*

God's Grace: God's unmerited favor or good will

I s God's grace sufficient enough? Is it sufficient enough to save you?
Save you to the point where you know that in spite of your situation
you are still a child of the King? God's grace prevents you and me from
determining, with our own mind, how much we need to say or do to receive
salvation. It is by God's grace that we are saved, not of our own doing, but
His grace alone (Eph. 2:8-9).

Is God's grace sufficient enough in weakness? Paul brought his weakness to the Lord. He pleaded with the Lord and hoped that the thorn in his
flesh would depart from him (2 Cor. 12:1-8). But God said unto Paul, "My
grace is sufficient for thee: for my strength is made perfect in weakness" (2
Cor. 12:9). Paul's spirit was quickened and he replied, "Most gladly therefore will I rather glory in my [weaknesses], that the power of Christ may
rest upon me. Therefore, I take pleasure in [weaknesses], in reproaches, in
necessities, in persecutions, in distresses for Christ's sake: for when I am
weak, then am I strong" (2 Cor. 12:9-10). God's grace is sufficient.

When Paul was weak, he made a decision to be strong in the name of
Jesus Christ. Like Paul, you can boast about the thorns in your life. You can
glorify God, and contrary to what your flesh may feel or see, you can yet
glorify Him. You can bless God's holy name. For when you glorify God,
the power of Christ will rest upon you. The power of Christ will allow you
to focus on those things that God has called you to do. It will allow you to
rejoice knowing that all things will work together for your good through
the power of Jesus Christ (Rom. 8:28).

Is God's grace sufficient enough to heal your situation? God's Word
states that He is the God that heals you, but is His grace, His unmerited

favor, enough for you to know that the healing has been completed and you can walk in your healing? Not just physical healing, but healing in all areas of your life. Jesus was "wounded for our transgressions, He was bruised for our iniquities: the chastisement of our peace was upon Him; and with His stripes [you] are healed" (Is. 53:4-5). God's grace is sufficient.

Is God's grace sufficient enough for worship and high praise? Has He not done enough for you, to you, and is He not yet still doing things for you? Has He not showered you with a love that is immeasurable and unconditional? His love is so limitless that

> *God's grace is sufficient.*

He sent His son, Jesus Christ, to save us. Jesus stretched Himself across a tree, hung until death, and then rose to live again with all power in His hands (Matt. 28:18). He now sits at the right hand of the Father interceding for you (Rom. 8:34). Jesus is your grace. His grace keeps you and gives you the desire to worship. For without God, without His grace, and without His favor, you would be lost and unfulfilled. Praise God for all that He has done in your life. He is worthy to be praised (Ps. 150). God's grace is sufficient.

Is God's grace sufficient enough to give you the courage to move forward in the midst of adversities? God's grace will change any situation. His grace is perfect and it is all powerful. His wonderful grace is Jesus Christ who was in the beginning (Jn. 1:1). The grace of God will do all that it is called to do. God's grace shields and covers you. God's awesome grace resides in those valleys that seem too deep to comprehend and too vast to see an end. His grace allows you to walk in awkward and uncomfortable places in your life and relationships. His amazing grace allows you to boast in your weaknesses knowing that when you are weak, afraid or troubled, God is made strong. God's grace is sufficient.

It is important for you to remember that grace is something you did not earn and there is nothing you can do to justify why you have it. God's grace keeps the power out of your hands and leaves it in His hands. His grace invites you to take His yoke when you are heavy laden (Matt. 11:28-30), and He will give you rest. God's awesome grace allows you to know that you are loved, favored, set apart, and protected by Him. Out of His love for you, you are blessed beyond measure, and you have received the gift of eternal life through His Son, Jesus Christ, who is full of grace and truth (Jn. 1:14).

Is God's grace sufficient? Yes, it is more than sufficient. Therefore, most gladly will we rather glory in our infirmities, that the power of Christ may rest upon us; for when we are weak, then we are strong in Jesus Christ, our Lord and Savior (2 Cor. 12:9-10).

Faith Affirmation: *Lord, Your grace is sufficient.*

Prayer: Lord, I thank You for today (Ps. 118:24). From the depths of my heart, I bless thee, and I praise thee (Ps. 145:2). You are my rock, my shield, my deliverer, and my God (Ps. 18:2). I thank You for Your awesome grace that is embracing me right now. I thank You that "[Your] strength is made perfect in [my] weakness" (2 Cor. 12:9). Your grace is sufficient!

Dear God Letter: Talk to God about your day. **God's grace is sufficient.**

Dear God,

GOD: IT'S AN EMERGENCY

As for me, I will call upon God; and the Lord shall save me (Ps. 55:16).

Life is full of many wonders, great times, challenges, and of course, emergencies. When people face emergencies or life threatening situations, they often call 911 – the emergency number. An emergency dispatcher picks up the call and immediately begins to listen to the caller and ask questions of the caller. The dispatcher wants to obtain information regarding the emergency situation and to quickly send the appropriate help (police department, fire department, ambulance, etc.). The dispatcher provides the individual with support and assists him/her with making the best of the situation. The individual often hopes and prays that the help will arrive on time.

As Christians, we also find ourselves in emergency or life threatening situations. We can't pay our bills. We've lost a loved one. We've lost our job or home. We're in an abusive relationship. The alcohol and/or drug use has become an addiction. Our happy home is being shaken at its foundation. Our dreams seem out of reach. The fear is tormenting us daily. The grief appears to have no end. The depression is consuming our life. The anxiety and uncontrollable thoughts are overwhelming. We don't know where to turn. We need help, and the local 911 number is not available for this type of distress. What we forget is that God's 911 emergency line is available for any type of distress and is open to all.

God is always available. You need not fear, for Jesus is your Lord and Savior. Anytime you are in distress, all you need to do is to open up your heart and mouth and call out the name of Jesus. He will immediately pick up. Out of His love for you, Jesus will intercede on your behalf with God the Father and send the perfect answer for your situation, and it will accomplish that which He has called it to do. His answer will prove to be "exceeding abundantly above all that [you] ask or think" (Eph. 3:20). Great is the Lord, who shall save you. Call **J-E-S-U-S** today. He is waiting for your call.

Faith Affirmation: *I will call on Jesus.*

Prayer: Lord, I thank You for creating this day, which is full of Your benefits and joy (Ps. 68:19; Ps. 118:24). "O LORD [my] Lord, how excellent is thy name in all the earth!" (Ps. 8:1). You are "[near] unto all them that call upon [You], to all that call upon [You] in truth" (Ps. 145:18). I will seek You and call upon Your name (Ps. 63:1-3), and I believe that You will answer (Ps. 138:3).

Dear God Letter: Talk to God about your day. Remember to call your **emergency number –J-E-S-U-S.**

Dear God,

Date:
Day #:

THE LAST RESORT OR GOD'S ANGEL

And David said to Saul, Let no man's heart fail because of [Goliath]; thy servant will go and fight this Philistine (1 Samuel 17:32).

Sometimes we appear to be someone's last resort; someone's angel. God sends us into the situation to bring forth His victory. David was the last resort for Saul and the armies of the living God. The men were so afraid of Goliath that when Goliath came to the battlefield, they fled with fear. David heard Goliath's threats and saw the men of the armies of Israel flee. In fact, he asked, "For who is this uncircumcised Philistine, that he would defy the armies of the living God?" (1 Sam. 17:26). Whoever he was, David had determined that Goliath was coming down by the power and might of God. David trusted in the Lord; therefore, he had no reason to fear Goliath (1 Sam. 17:32-37).

The men's fear and lack of trust in God had led them to accept defeat and the shame that came along with defeat. They were willing to lose all that God had given them in order not to lose their life. They had placed more value on their lives than the power and might of God. They hoped someone from the army would stand up and fight—anybody.

In the midst of their lack of faith and trust in God, God still made a way out of what appeared to be a situation that had no way out, except through death and defeat. God brought forth David and the men used him as their last resort. The men had become so desperate that they were willing to send an adolescent boy to fight Goliath. At least the men who survived the battle would be able to declare that they stood up to Goliath, but he was much too strong and skillful.

God also calls us to be someone's last resort, someone's angel of God. We have all heard the stories of someone receiving help when there appeared to be no way out. I have heard about the time someone spoke to

35

a stranger and that person revealed that she just couldn't go on. God gave the person a listening ear and a word of love and peace that blessed the stranger's life. The person stated, "God has sent me an angel." Or, the time someone was deeply saddened and grieved, and God quickened his mate's spirit, and she spoke God's word

God has sent me an angel.

of encouragement, love, and life, and he asked his wife, "How did you know my deepest pain and fear." She responded, "God revealed it to me and requested that I speak to you today." Or, the time a woman called her friend that she had not spoken to for years, only to find out that her friend had been diagnosed with a serious illness. The woman spoke forth God's words of healing and comfort. Her friend cried out, "Thank You Lord, for sending Your angel." Or, the time some folks were out giving food to the homeless and one of the women who was homeless stated, "I prayed to God this morning and asked Him where I was going to get my next meal. You are an angel sent by God." Some may say you're their last resort while others may say you're God's angel. God will say, "Well done, [my] good and faithful servant" (Matt. 25:21).

Faith Affirmation: *I will allow the Lord to use me.*

Prayer: Lord, I thank You for this day (Ps. 118:24) and all that You have done me. I will "sing forth the honor of [Your] name" (Ps. 66:2). It is Your desire that none of Your children's hearts shall fail. I accept my assignment to do Your will and to speak Your word of love, hope, faith, and deliverance. I thank You for Your divine power, confidence, and victory.

Dear God Letter: Talk to God about your day. God will use you to help His people, and some will say "you are their **last resort,**" while others will say, **"you are God's angel."**

Dear God,

SOMETIMES

*Humble yourselves therefore under the mighty hand of God, that He
may exalt you in due time: Casting all your care upon Him; for He
careth for you (1 Pet. 5:6-7).*

S ometimes life seems more unreal than real.
Cry out to the Lord as David did, and He will strengthen your soul and
give you an abundance of will (Ps. 62).

Sometimes when it seems as if your life is in the eye of the storm, cry out
to the Lord for only He has the power to calm the heavy wind and rain
(Ps.107:28-30).

Sometimes a situation in your life will become a mountain that you can't
seem to climb. Have faith and hold on to your hope in the Lord; knowing
that with God all things are possible (Lk. 1:37).

Sometimes your enemies may attack you all at once, but God shall lift up
a standard against them (Isa. 59:19).

Sometimes the adversities of life seem as if they are getting the best of you.
Pause and encourage yourself in the Lord. You are more than a conqueror
through Christ Jesus who loves you (Rom. 8:37).

Sometimes, people will fail you, but keep your trust in the Lord for He
never fails (Ps. 118:8; Jer. 31:3).

Sometimes your 'sometimes' feel as if they are going to last forever, 'but
they that wait upon the LORD shall renew their strength; they shall mount
up with wings as eagles; they shall run, and not be weary; and they shall
walk, and not faint" (Isa. 40:31). They shall be blessed!

Call on God. He loves you, and He is always in your sometimes. **Always**

Faith Affirmation: *God is in my "sometimes."*

Prayer: Lord, I thank You for considering me as You created this day. I have committed to rejoicing and being glad each day (Ps. 118:24). "Because [Your] lovingkindness is better than life, my lips shall praise [You]" (Ps. 63:3). I thank You for being in my "sometimes" and for loving me in spite of my "sometimes."

Dear God Letter: Talk to God about your day. Cast your care on the Lord; not **sometimes** but **always**.

Dear God,

Date:
Day #:

REJOICE IN GOD'S DAY!

This is the day which the Lord hath made; we will rejoice and be glad in it (Ps. 118:24).

T ake the time to enjoy and rejoice in the day that God has made for you. It is the only day that God has given to you. He may give you tomorrow, but that will be His decision. Surely, you can plan for tomorrow but you must live, rejoice and be glad today. Establish yourself to live in the now—to live in this day.

I rejoice knowing that God loves me more than I can comprehend, and His love for me is everlasting to everlasting (Jn. 3:16; Jn. 15:13-14).
I rejoice knowing that God is "with [me] always, even unto the ends of the world" (Matt. 28:20).
God lives within me, and He is at the heart of every matter (1 Cor. 3:16; Ps. 73:26).

Hallelujah!

I rejoice knowing that there is nothing too hard for God (Gen. 18:14).
I rejoice knowing that He will not give me more than I can bear (1 Pet. 5:7).
I rejoice knowing that "in [God's] favor is life: weeping may endure for a night, but joy cometh in the morning" (Ps. 30:5).
I rejoice knowing that the "battle is the LORD's!" (1 Sam. 17:47).
God is Mighty!

I rejoice knowing that God is "able to do exceeding abundantly above all that [I] ask or think, according to the power that worketh in [me]" (Eph. 3:20).
"For with God all things are possible" (Mk. 10:27).
I rejoice for the "joy of the Lord is [my] strength" (Neh. 8:10).

I rejoice knowing that "faithful is He that calleth [me], who also will do it" (1 Thess. 5:24).
God is Awesome!

Faith Affirmation: *I shall rejoice and be glad.*

Prayer: Father, I thank You for another day to sing unto You a new song of praise (Ps. 96:1). From the depths of my heart, I give You the highest praise. "Great [are You Lord], and greatly to be praised; and [Your] greatness is unsearchable" (Ps. 145:3). I thank You for establishing a trusting and loving relationship with me. I will rejoice and be glad in You.

Dear God Letter: Talk to God about your day. Remember to live and **rejoice in God's day.**

Dear God,

EVEN IF

Shadrach, Meshach and Abednego answered and said to the king. . . If it be so, our God whom we serve is able to deliver us from the burning fiery furnace, and he will deliver us out of thine hand, O king. But if not, be it known unto thee, O king, that we will not serve thy gods, nor worship the golden image which thou hast set up (Dan. 3:16-18).

The Babylonians under the rule of King Nebuchadnezzar had captured the Hebrew boys, Hananiah, Mishael, Azariah, and Daniel, during the fall of Judah. The king chose Hananiah (God Is Gracious), Mishael (God Is Without Equal), Azariah (The Lord Is My Helper) and Daniel (God Is My Judge) to become a part of an elite group of captives "in whom was no blemish, but well favored, and skillful in all wisdom, and cunning in knowledge, and understanding science. . ." (Dan. 1:4). This elite group would be required to become immersed in the Babylonian culture and do those things that benefited the Babylonian kingdom.

In the face of being stripped of their identities, the boys held steadfast to their God-given identities. The boys purposed in their heart that they would hold on to their Jewish identity and live a life that was acceptable and pleasing unto God. The Hebrew boys remained committed to their people and God. They chose to live by God's law and presented for all to see, an "even if" attitude.

Even if King Nebuchadnezzar changed their Hebrew names to Shadrach, Meshach, Abednego and Belteshazzar, which represented the Babylonians gods, they would hold on to their Hebrew names. They would call each other by their birth names. These names served to remind them of "whose they were." These names tied them to their existence and destiny.

> *We all need an "even if" attitude.*

Even if the boys were taught the Babylonian ways and given high positions, they would not eat the meat of the Babylonians, nor worship their gods. "But Daniel purposed in his heart that he would not defile himself with the portion of the king's meat, nor with the wine which he drank. . ." (Dan. 1:8). The Lord blessed the faithfulness of the Hebrew boys and showed them favor among the eunuchs and the king. Even if they received the favor of the king, they would not worship the Babylonian gods nor bow before the golden image that the king had made. They would only worship God, the God of Abraham, Isaac, and Jacob.

Even if, the king chose to cast them into the fiery furnace because they would not bow and worship his idol golden image, they would hold on to God. They would declare to King Nebuchadnezzar, "If it be so, our God whom we serve is able to deliver us from the burning fiery furnace, and He will deliver us out of thine hand, O king. But if not, be it known unto thee, O king, that we will not serve thy gods, nor worship the golden image which thou hast set up" (Dan. 3:17-18).

We all need an "even if" attitude. It is God who is the author and finisher of our success. As a believer, an "even if" attitude shows your unshakeable confidence and faith in God. Your "even if" attitude strengthens your belief and commitment to God. Seek God diligently, with an open heart and confess your "even if" attitude today. Let's stand today and declare-

Lord,

Even if . . .	I will call out the name of Jesus Christ (Ps. 124:8).
Even if . . .	I will praise Your holy name (Ps. 113).
Even if . . .	I know that You love me (Jn. 3:16; Jn. 15:13-14).
Even if . . .	I know that You have called me (Phil. 1:6).
Even if . . .	I will have faith in You (Mk. 11:22).
Even if . . .	I know that it is You who heals (Isa. 53:5).
Even if . . .	I know that You have a plan for my situation and life (Jer. 29:11).
Even if . . .	I know that Your "[word] shall not return unto [You] void, but it will accomplish that which [You] please. . ." (Isa. 55:11).
Even if . . .	I know that You will provide for all my needs (Matt. 6:31-33; Phil. 4:19).
Even if . . .	You are "able to do exceeding abundantly above all that [I] ask or think, according to the power that worketh in [me]" (Eph. 3:20).

Even if . . .	I will walk upright with You (Ps. 84:11).
Even if . . .	I will count it all joy (Jas. 1:2).
Even if . . .	I know that the You are my Shepherd (Ps. 23:1).
Even if . . .	I know that the You are I AM THAT I AM in my life (Ex. 3:14).
Even if . . .	I know that You will never leave me nor forsake me (Matt. 28:20).
Even if . . .	You will remain my rock, my shield and my protector (Ps. 31:3).
Even if . . .	I know that I have never "seen the righteous forsaken, nor [Your] seed begging for bread" (Ps. 37:25).
Even if . . .	I know that Your joy cometh in the morning (Ps. 30:5).
Even if . . .	I will not be moved. I will stand on the Rock from which my help cometh (Ps. 61:2).
Even if . . .	I know that nothing shall separate me from Your love (Rom. 8:35-39).
Even if . . .	I will keep my heart with You (Ps. 119:11; Ps. 28:7).

Faith Affirmation: *Even if, I will serve the Lord.*

Prayer: Father, I thank You for this day (Ps. 118:24). I thank You for loving me. I will "declare [Your] glory among the [unbelievers], [Your] wonders among all people" (Ps. 96:3). I will give You the glory due Your name (Ps. 96:8). I thank You for my "even if" attitude, and I plan to hold on to it. It is a heartfelt attitude that expresses my love and commitment to You.

Dear God Letter: Talk to God about your day. Even though some situations may appear to be a fiery furnace, maintain an **"even if"** attitude. God has the final answer.

Dear God,

Date:
Day #:

A LOVING RELATIONSHIP

*I am the good shepherd: the good shepherd giveth his life for the
sheep. . . No man taketh [my life] from me, but I lay it down of myself.
I have power to lay it down, and I have power to take it again. This
commandment have I received of my Father (Jn. 10:11-18).*

God loves us so much that He sent His Son to save the world – to save
you–to save us. Jesus, the only begotten Son of God, lay down His
life for the world—for you and me (Jn. 3:16). While we were yet sinners,
He died in our place (Rom. 5:8). Jesus suffered in the flesh and bore our sins
(1 Jn. 2:2) so that we could be reconciled to the Father and receive God's
gift of eternal life (Jn. 3:16; Eph. 2:8-9). "He is the propitiation for our sins:
and not for ours only, but also for the sins of the whole world" (1 Jn. 2:2).

> "Then delivered he Him therefore unto them to be
> crucified. And they took Jesus, and led him away. And
> He bearing His cross went forth into a place called the
> place of a skull, which is called in the Hebrew Golgotha:
> Where they crucified Him, and two others with Him, on
> either side one, and Jesus in the midst. . . Now there
> stood by the cross of Jesus His mother, and His mother's
> sister, Mary the wife of Cleophas, and Mary Magdalene.
> When Jesus therefore saw His mother, and the disciple
> standing by, whom He loved, He saith unto his mother,
> Woman, behold thy son! . . . After this, Jesus knowing
> that all things were now accomplished, that the scripture
> might be fulfilled, saith, I thirst. . . When Jesus therefore
> had received the vinegar, He said, It is finished: and He
> bowed his head, and gave up the ghost" (Jn. 19:16-30).

This was not the end. On the third day, Jesus rose with all glory and power in His hands. He now sits on the right hand of the Father, as our loving advocate, communicating with God the Father on our behalf (Rom. 8:34). With the death and resurrection of Jesus, God the Father gave us God the Holy Spirit so that He would always abide with us (Jn. 14:16) – now that's love.

Faith Affirmation: *I have a loving relationship with the Father.*

Prayer: Father, this is the day that You have made for me (Ps. 118:24). I will bless Your name forever (Ps. 115:18). I thank You for Your unconditional love. I thank You for sending Your Son, Jesus Christ, so that I can have a loving relationship with You. I want You to fill me with more of You. It is my heart's desire to be more dependent on You and to reach the expected end that You have for me. I love You.

Dear God Letter: Talk to God about your day. God is with you always and desires for you to draw closer to Him and to enjoy a **loving relationship** with Him.

Dear God,

Date:
Day #:

LIFE CHANGING MOMENTS

. . . and so will I go unto the king, which is not according to the law: and if I perish, I perish (Est. 4:16).

Esther was an ordinary woman who faced loss early in her life. Her parents died and her uncle, Mordecai, raised her. Mordecai, a man of God, saw Esther's beauty and potential so much so that when King Ahasuerus, the king of Persia, called for a new wife, he believed that Esther could become the next queen. Esther was brought unto the king's house to the custody of Hegai, keeper of the women (Est. 2:8). She pleased Hegai, and she obtained kindness from him. "And Esther found favor in the sight of all of them that looked upon her. So Esther was taken unto King Ahasuerus into his house. . . And the king loved Esther above all the women, and she obtained grace and favor in his sight more than all the virgins; so that he set the royal crown upon her head, and made her queen" (Est. 2:15-17). What a life changing journey and moment. This was just the beginning of her life changing moment.

After becoming the queen, she was asked to risk her life to save her uncle and the other Jewish people who were living in the Persian region. God had called her to be the queen and the woman who would intervene on behalf of the Jewish people. The story goes something like this. "All the king's servants, that were in the king's gate, bowed, and reverenced Haman [one of the king's high officials]; for the king had so commanded concerning him. But Mordecai bowed not, nor did him reverence" (Est. 3:2). When Haman saw that Mordecai would not bow nor reverence him, he became furious. He sought to kill Mordecai and destroy all the Jews that were throughout the kingdom of Ahasuerus (Est. 3:6). When Mordecai learned of Haman's plot, "[he] rent his clothes and put on sackcloth with ashes, and went out into the midst of the city, and cried with a loud and bitter cry" (Est. 4:1). In response to Haman's threat to destroy them, the

Jewish people also mourned, fasted, wept, wailed, and lay in sack clothes all in hopes that the Lord would hear their cries and save them.

Esther heard of her uncle's great mourning and the mourning of the Jewish people. She sent a message to Mordecai and asked why so much grief. Mordecai told Esther of the king's decree. He also requested that she go see the king on the Jews' behalf. Esther sent a message back saying that she had not been asked to come before the king in the last 30 days. Basically, she could not go before him unless he called her. Therefore, she could not speak to the king about his decree. Mordecai answered Esther, "Think not with thyself that thou shalt escape in the king's house, more than all of the Jews. For if thou altogether holdest thy peace at this time, then shall there enlargement and deliverance arise to the Jews from another place; but thou and thy father's house shall be destroyed: and who knoweth whether thou art come to the kingdom for such a time as this?" (Est. 4:13-14).

Mordecai's words caused Esther to ponder and recognize that she had not become queen by accident. God had chosen her. His words stirred up her spirit of faith and courage. God had chosen her for such a time as this, and she would go before the king. If she perished, she would perish (Est. 4:16), but not because she did not trust the only true God. Esther's faith and courage allowed her to fulfill her divine purpose. What a life changing moment!

Faith Affirmation: *I have been prepared by God for such a time as this.*

Prayer: Lord, I thank You for today. My heart seeks after You. You are my love, my peace, and my joy. You are everything to me. I may face unexpected situations and temptations, but I will trust that I am covered by Your favor (Ps. 5:12). Lord, I accept that I have been called for such a time as this (Est. 4:14). I thank You in advance for the courage to make the right choice and to fulfill my divine purpose.

Dear God Letter: Talk to God about your day. Remember that during your journey, you will have **life changing moments**.

Dear God,

GOD OUR REFUGE AND STRENGTH

God is our refuge and strength, a very present help in trouble (Ps. 46:1).

G od requires that we are still or at rest knowing that He is our refuge, our strength, and our fortress (Ps. 91:2). However, sometimes, we get so restless and impatient to the point that we decide to take matters into our own hands. All we can see are the troubled and roaring waters. Yet, when we take matters into our own hands, we leave ourselves and others vulnerable to Satan's wicked schemes and attacks.

When David was on the run for his life, he became quite fearful. Yes, the same David that slew Goliath. No one is perfect. One time, in particular, he fled to Nob, the city of priests. He lied to the priest, Ahimelech, and told him that King Saul had sent him on business. David requested that the priest provides him and his men with food and shelter. Oh, the tangled webs we weave!

These amenities provided David and his men with an opportunity to rebuild their strength and push forward in their quest to escape death at the hands of Saul and his army. The priest's obedience to David placed him and his city in grave danger; the danger

> *God is our refuge and strength.*

David secretly knew would cause them hardship if Saul found out.

Saul found out that the priest helped David. Saul and the men of his army rode to Nob to confront Ahimelech. The priest explained that he had provided the food not knowing that David was on the run from King Saul. Had he known, he would not have provided David and his men with the provisions. Nonetheless, Saul in his fit of rage ordered the priest, the women, children, and animals killed (1 Sam. 22:6-19). David did not antic- ipate that Saul would go as far as to kill the priest and the people. Priests were holy men called of God. Saul, in all of his rage and craziness, was still the Lord's anointed. He wouldn't dare!

Once we step out of God's will, we give Satan room to steal, kill, and destroy (Jn. 10:10). Our focus must always remain on God. Make the decision today to repent of your sin of not trusting God and fearing what man can do unto you (Ps. 118:6). Make the decision to trust in the Lord. Ask God to show you how to resolve your fears—family or relationship conflict, work concerns, self-doubt, financial woes, and anything else that is troubling you. Don't take off walking, skipping, jogging or running without God. Keep your eyes off your troubles and seek refuge in God.

Faith Affirmation: *I will tell the truth and trust the Lord to do the rest.*

Prayer: Father, I thank You for another day to acknowledge "How excellent is [Your] name in all [the] earth! (Ps. 8:1). "I will love thee, O LORD, . . . my rock, and my fortress, and my deliverer; my God, my strength, in whom I will trust; my buckler, and the horn of my salvation, and my high tower. I will call upon [You], who is worthy to be praised: so shall I be saved from mine enemies" (Ps. 18:1-3).

Dear God Letter: Talk to God about your day. God is your **refuge, strength, and fortress**, and you need not fear.

Dear God,

YOUR TESTIMONY

David said moreover, The Lord that delivered me out of the paw of the lion, and out of the paw of the bear, He will deliver me out of the hand of this Philistine (1 Sam. 17:37).

Look to your past and pull out your testimony. It is your testimony that builds your unshakeable faith and confidence in God. This unshakeable faith is your shield, which is needed on the battlefield. Your testimony is evidence of God's awesome power and reminds you that there is nothing too hard for God (Gen. 18:14). Your testimony will lead you and others to continue to praise and worship God.

David's relationship with God built his faith and confidence in the mighty power of God. When David was brought before King Saul to tell him that he would defeat Goliath, he spoke boldly to Saul and confirmed that he would go against Goliath and defeat him. Goliath, the giant, who stood over 9 feet tall and had come from a lineage of skilled warriors. You know Goliath, the champion warrior and giant, who had sent the armies of the living God running in fear. Saul replied to David, "Thou art not able to go against this Philistine to fight with him: for thou art but a youth, and he a man of war from his youth" (1 Sam. 17:33). David replied with his testimony,

> "Thy servant kept his father's sheep and there came a lion, and a bear, and took a lamb out of the flock: And I went out after him and smote him, and delivered it out of his mouth: and when he arose against me, I caught him by his beard, and smote him, and slew him. Thy servant slew both the lion and the bear: and this uncircumcised Philistine shall be as one of them, seeing he hath defied the armies of the living God. David said, "Moreover, the Lord that delivered me out of the paw of the lion, and out of the paw of the bear,

55

will deliver me out of the hand of this Philistine. And Saul said unto David, Go, and the Lord be with thee" (1 Sam. 17:35-37).

Saul knew David spoke the truth about the mighty power of God. He had his own testimony about what God had done for him. Therefore, Saul no longer questioned David's ability to defeat Goliath.

We all have a testimony of what God has done for us. We have also heard the testimony of others. Take the time to recall your testimony and meditate on it. Bring your remembrance of what God has done for you to mind and keep it there. Thank and praise God for what He has done for you. Share your testimony with others (Ps. 119:24). The next time Satan rises up against you, present your testimony. It is the faith weapon that you will need above all to keep you strong in the midst of spiritual warfare.

Faith Affirmation: *I will use my testimony to confirm God's power and might.*

Prayer: Lord, I thank You for today (Ps. 118:24). I will praise You with my whole heart (Ps. 111:1). I will use my testimony to stay focused on You. I will use my testimony to stand in the wicked days. I will use my testimony to rejoice and be glad in You. "My flesh and heart may fail, but [You are] the strength of my heart, and my portion forever" (Ps. 73:26). I thank You for my shield of faith testimony.

Dear God Letter: Talk to God about your day. Delight in **your testimonies;** they are good counsel.

Dear God,

LOOK TO THE ONE

I will lift up mine eyes unto the hills, from whence cometh my help (Ps. 121:1).

In all situations, you must find the strength to look to God from whom your help and deliverance come (Ps. 121:1-2). Look forward to what God has planned for you. Look forward to what God has in store for you. He only has what is good, right and just planned for your situation and future. Don't look back and think if I would have or if I could have. God has brought you out to take you to greater things. You may not understand, but as the songwriter wrote, "You'll understand it better by and by."

We have all had a situation that we didn't understand why it had to happen that way. Why couldn't you stay on that job? Why couldn't you stay in that relationship? Why do you have a life threatening illness? Why did your friend have to die? Why are you struggling so hard to pay your bills? Why? Why? Why? Even though you are worried about your situation, you must look to God "from whence cometh your help." God will make a way. Take your eyes off the situation and seek God for His answer. Seek comfort from the Holy Spirit and rejoice in the name of Jesus knowing that it will all work out for your good.

Don't look back questioning yourself or trying to grab hold of your old stuff. God will renew and restore all that you have lost. Turn into your present moment and acknowledge that God has ordered your steps to your next promised land. God loves you, and He

Keep your eyes on God.

is with you always (Matt. 28:20). He is Jehovah Shammah, the One who is Always There. He is El Shaddai, the All Sufficient One. He is Jehovah Rohi, the Lord your Shepherd. He is everything you need Him to be and so much more.

Don't look back. Don't turn into a pillar of salt as Lot's wife did when she looked back into the cities of Sodom and Gomorrah (Gen. 19:15-26). One look can send you back into a relationship that leads to your spiritual death. One look can keep you in a job that you know God called you to leave. One look can freeze you in your fears and self-doubt, causing you to be imprisoned in depression. One look can allow Satan to deceive you into believing that the grass is greener on the other side. One look can blind you from realizing your full potential. The bottom line is that one look can keep you from obeying God's command.

Look forward to God from where all your blessings flow. Look to your next exciting moment. Look to your new opportunities. Keep your eyes on God, as He guides you to another good place in life. Keep your eyes on God as He mends your relationships and heals your body. Keep your eyes on Jehovah Jireh, the One who will make provisions for you. Reach deep into your heart and call on the name of Jesus. Thank and praise God for bringing you forward. He is the author and finisher of your success – your hopes and dreams.

Faith Affirmation: *I will look to God and allow Him to order my steps.*

Prayer: Father, I thank You for this day (Ps. 118:24). You are good, and Your mercy endures forever (Ps. 118:1). "Thou art my God, and I will praise thee: thou art my God, I will exalt thee" (Ps. 118:28). You are my provider, strength, deliverer, and salvation (Ps. 18:2). Lord, You are my everything. I will look only to You from where perfect help and direction comes (Ps. 121:1). I shall live, move, and breathe with You forever (Acts 17:28).

Dear God Letter: Talk to God about your day. Remember to **look to the One who will deliver you.**

Dear God,

GOOD THOUGHTS

Finally, brethren, whatsoever things are true, whatsoever things are honest, whatsoever things are just, whatsoever things are pure, whatsoever things are lovely, whatsoever things are of good report; if there be any virtue, and if there be any praise, think on these things (Phil. 4:8).

G od asks us to think on those thoughts that are good (Phil. 4:8). He wants us to think about the "good stuff," and how excellent He is in our lives and in all the earth (Ps. 8:1). Take the time to think about God's victories in your life. Think about a moment that brought you peace, joy, happiness, healing or comfort. Hold on to those thoughts. Meditate on those good thoughts. Let them rest in your mind, body, heart, and soul.

The more you take the time to think on good thoughts, the more your attitude will become positive. You will develop a positive attitude and a heart that trusts God. You will begin to feel more upbeat. You will also begin to focus on the good things in life and become more appreciative of what God has done for you. In the midst of everyday life, you will find God's peace. The colors of the flowers will

Think on good thoughts.

become more vibrant and beautiful. The smell of the flowers will become sweeter. More things in your life will be amusing and funny. One of my sisters who didn't even tell many jokes is now just full of jokes and laughter. You will freely give comments and words of encouragement to yourself and others. You will begin to see yourself as God sees you, a beautiful person made in His own image and likeness (Gen. 1:26; Ps. 139:14).

When Satan tries to step in with one of his lies, you will not receive it. You will call on the name of Jesus. You will think about "how excellent is [His] name is in all the earth!" (Ps. 8:1). You will look the deception straight in the eye and say, "The Lord has won this battle. This is the day which the Lord hath made; [I] will rejoice and be glad in it" (Ps. 118:24). You will thank the Lord for allowing you to recognize Satan's deception. You will think on those thoughts that are good; those thoughts that strengthen you and draw you closer to your divine purpose and closer to God, your Lord and Savior.

Faith Affirmation: *I will think good thoughts.*

Prayer: Lord, I give thanks to You for this day (Ps. 118:24). "Every day will I bless thee; and I will praise [Your] name forever and ever" (Ps. 145:2). I will delight myself in You (Ps. 37:4) You are great and greatly to be praised (Ps. 145:3). I will do what is pleasing unto You (Prov. 16:7). I will think on those things that are honest, just, pure, lovely and of good report (Phil. 4:8). I will think about You. I love You, Lord.

Dear God Letter: Talk to God about your day. Remember to think **good thoughts,** those things that are true, honest, just, pure, lovely, and of good report.

Dear God,

IN A SPLIT SECOND

Behold, I show you a mystery; we shall not all sleep, but we shall all be changed, in a moment, in the twinkling of an eye, at the last trumpet: for the trumpet shall sound, and the dead shall be raised incorruptible, and we shall be changed (1 Cor. 15:51-52).

God will move in *a split second and a twinkling of an eye.* I'm reminded of the story of Lazarus. Lazarus became quite ill. His sisters, Mary and Martha, sent a message to Jesus, saying that Lazarus, the one You love is sick (Jn. 11:3). When Jesus heard the news, he finished his work and then went with his disciples to Judea, the home of Mary, Martha, and Lazarus. When Jesus arrived, Lazarus had "lain in the grave four days already" (Jn. 11:17). Martha went to Jesus and said,

> "If you [had] been here, my brother had not died. But I know, that even now, whatsoever thou wilt ask of God, God will give it thee. . . Jesus said unto her, I am the resurrection, and the life: he that believeth in me, though he were dead, yet shall he live: And whosoever liveth and believeth in me shall never die. Believest thou this? She saith unto Him, Yea, Lord: I believe that thou are the Christ, the Son of God. . . And when she had so said, she went her way. . ."
> (Jn. 11:20-28).

Mary and Martha were both very sad and troubled by the death of their brother. "When Jesus therefore saw [Mary] weeping, and the Jews also weeping which came with her, "He groaned in the spirit, and was troubled. . . Jesus wept" (Jn. 11:33-35). Mary and Martha knew that Jesus loved Lazarus and if he had been in town, their brother would not have died. Martha also knew that whatsoever she asked of God, He would give it to her. But her brother was dead. Did the "whatsoever" include bringing her brother back to life? Lazarus had lay dead for four days.

Jesus requested that the Jews take away the stone where Lazarus lay dead. Martha said unto Him: "by this time he stinketh: for he hath been dead four days" (Jn. 11:39). Jesus replied, "Said I not unto thee, that, if thou wouldest believe, thou shouldest see the glory of God? Then they took away the stone from the place where the dead was laid. And Jesus lifted up his eyes, and said, Father, I thank thee that thou hast heard me. And I knew that thou hearest me always: but because of the people which stand by I said it, that they may believe that thou hast sent me. And when He thus had spoken, He cried with a loud voice, Lazarus, come forth. And he that was dead came forth . . . [and] many of the Jews...believed on Him" (Jn. 11:40-45). In a split second and a twinkling of an eye, Jesus responded to Mary and Martha's heartfelt faith and raised Lazarus from the dead and those that were there believed on Him.

We all confront different life situations that seem to bring us grief, discomfort, doubt, fear and so on. These situations often have different durations and leave us wondering if we're going to make it. Don't focus on the

God will intervene in a split second.

duration of your situation; focus on the delivering power of God. If you approach God with your heartfelt faith, you will make it; "for the battle is the Lord's" (1 Sam. 17:47). God will send peace and direction for your next step. God will open the door to your next job. He will mend your relationship. He will show you how to love your children. God will heal your body, and He will heal your inner hurts and wounds. He will do exceeding abundantly above all that you can ask, think or imagine (Eph. 3:20). Put your heart, faith, and situation in God's hands. He knows the days, hours, minutes and seconds of your situation. He knows what is best for you. Call on the name of Jesus. He will intervene – *in a split second and a twinkling of an eye*. God loves you!

Faith Affirmation: *I will keep my heart and mind set on Jesus.*

Prayer: Lord, I thank You for this day; another day to honor Your name and to rejoice and be glad (Ps. 118:24). I will forever praise Your name (Ps. 148:5). "[Your] glory is above the earth and heaven" (Ps. 148:13). You are "the resurrection, and the life" (Jn. 11:25). It is You who has the power to give eternal life (Eph. 2:8-9). I will wait on You (Isa. 40:31). You will move in my life in a split second and a twinkling of an eye. Hallelujah!

Dear God Letter: Talk to God about your day. Remember to live each day knowing that **God will intervene in a split second.**

Dear God,

Date:
Day #:

I KNOW THIS VERY THING

Being confident of this very thing, that He which hath begun a good work in you will perform it until the day of Jesus Christ (Phil. 1:6).

When you speak and pray remember to confess what you know regarding the love and power of God. Lord, I know that You are love, and You love me. I also know that "all things work together for good to them that love God, to them who are called according to [Your] purpose" (Rom. 8:28). Lord, my finances are limited but I am confident of this very thing, that You will bring me prosperity. "The earth is the LORD's, and the fullness thereof. . ." (Ps. 24:1). The physician has diagnosed me with a terminal illness. I am confident of this very thing, that "with [Your] stripes [I am] healed" (Isa. 53:5). I'm walking with You each and every day and feel Your presence. I am confident of this very thing, that I know You are "with me always, even unto the end of the world" (Matt. 28:20). I am also confident of this very thing, that You came "that [I] might have life, and that [I] might have it more abundantly" (Jn. 10:10).

Remember to speak the words of the Lord. His words are "spirit, and they are life" (Jn. 6:63). You must hold on to the Word of God and live a life full of liberty and joy. Each day confess the goodness of God and all that He has done and will do for you. Don't forget to thank Him for you. You are His workmanship (Eph. 2:10) and created in His image and likeness (Gen. 1:26-27). You must be "confident of this very thing, that He which hath begun a good work in you will perform it until the day of Jesus Christ" (Phil. 1:6).

Faith Affirmation: *God has begun a good work in me, and He will complete it (Phil. 1:6).*

Prayer: Lord, I thank You for today. "Every day will I bless thee; and I will praise [Your] name for ever and ever" (Ps. 145:2). You formed me in my mother's womb and sanctified and called me (Jer. 1:5). Lord, "[You] know the thoughts that [You] think toward [me], thoughts of peace, and not of evil, to give [me] an expected end" –divine destiny (Jer. 29:11). Therefore, I am confident of this very thing that You have "begun a good work in me and will perform it unto the day of Jesus Christ" (Phil. 1:6).

Dear God Letter: Talk to God about your day. Remember to be **confident of this very thing** that God's good work in you will be performed.

Dear God,

Date:
Day #:

GOD IS IN EVERY SEASON

To every thing there is a season, and a time to every purpose under the heaven (Eccles. 3:1).

"To every thing there is a season, and a time to every purpose under the heaven" (Eccles. 3:1). It is always your season no matter how you feel or choose to accept it. It is God who calls each season, and He is in each one with you. God allows each season to happen in your life to benefit you and those He has called you to bless. In every season, you must seek God. In every season, you must look for the good and experience the good; for every good and perfect thing comes from God (Jas. 1:17).

If you realize that God allows the season in your life and is present with you in the season, you will be able to grow and benefit. Some seasons may seem as if they are full of stress and demands. God will not give you more than you can bear (1 Pet. 5:7). It may be a season full of changes. Just hold on to the Jesus, He is the "same yesterday, and today, and forever" (Heb. 13:8). Your season could be full of peace, joy, and gladness. The peace of the Lord surpasses all understanding (Phil. 4:7). The Lord's "presence is fullness of joy; at [His] right hand there are pleasures for evermore" (Ps. 16:11). Whatever the season, God has called it; therefore, it will benefit you, build your Christ-like character and draw you closer to your calling and divine purpose.

In Ecclesiastes 3:14-15, the author writes, "I know that, whatsoever God doeth, it shall be forever: nothing can be put to it, nor any thing taken from it: and God doeth it, that men should fear before Him. That which hath been is now; and that which is to be hath already been; and God requireth that which is past." Praise God!

Faith Affirmation: *God is in this season with me.*

71

Prayer: Lord, I thank You for this day (Ps. 118:24) and this season (Eccles. 3). You are "great, and greatly to be praised" (Ps. 96:4). You have sovereign and divine authority. You created the heavens and earth and all that is within it (Ps. 24:1). I will stay the course and experience the season that You have called for my life. I know that all things will work together for my good according to Your purpose (Rom. 8:28).

Dear God Letter: Talk to God about your day. Remember **God is in every season with you.**

Dear God,

WHAT IS YOUR REPORT?

And they told him, and said, We came unto the land whither thou sentest
us, and surely it floweth with milk and honey; and this is the fruit of it.
Nevertheless the people be strong that dwell in the land. . .and moreover
we saw the children of Anak there . . . And Caleb stilled the people before
Moses, and said, Let us go up at once, and possess it; for we are well able
to overcome it (Num. 13:27-30).

G od led Moses and the people of Israel to Canaan, the ancient name
of the land of Israel, and told Moses that the people were to go and
possess the land. "And the Lord [spoke] unto Moses, saying, Send thou
men, that they may search the land of Canaan, which I give unto the children of Israel. . ." (Num. 13:1-2). Moses sent spies, the heads of the children of Israel, to check out the land. When the spies had checked out the
land and its inhabitants, they brought back word unto Moses and Aaron, and
unto the entire congregation. They showed them the fruit of the land. They
reported that the land was flowing with milk and honey (Num. 13:27-28).
This information excited the people. However, they also reported that the
people were strong; the cities were walled and great, and there were giants
of Anak in the land (Num. 13:26-28). This part of the report caused fear
among the people. "And Caleb [one of the spies] stilled the people before
Moses, and said, Let us go up at once, and possess it; for we are well able
to overcome it" (Num. 13:30). Caleb saw the giants, the walled cities, and
the strong people. He also knew God and trusted that He would fulfill His
promise that they would possess the land. Caleb had unfaltering faith in God,
and God's mighty power and promises.

However, the other heads of the children of Israel who went up with
Caleb said,

> "We be not able to go up against the people; for they are
> stronger than we. And they brought up an evil report of the

73

land which they had searched unto the children of Israel, saying, 'The land, through which we have gone to search it, is a land that eateth up the inhabitants thereof; and all the people that we saw in it are men of a great stature. And there we saw the giants, the sons of Anak, which come of the giants: and we were in our own sight as grasshoppers, and so we were in their sight.' And the entire congregation lifted up their voice, and cried; and the people wept that night" (Num. 13:31-33; 14:1).

The people believed the negative report of the men rather than the positive report of Caleb. The people murmured and complained against Moses and Aaron and questioned God's authority and promise. They became so afraid that they proposed to return to Egypt, the land that they had begged God to deliver them from. Moses and Aaron sought the Lord and others prayed to God. Moses and Aaron spoke to the people, "If the Lord delight in us, then He will bring us into this land, and give it us; a land which floweth with milk and honey. Only rebel not against the Lord, neither fear ye the people of the land; for they are bread for us: their defense is departed from them, and the Lord is with us: fear them not" (Num. 14:8-9). Yet, the people still turned from God and rebelled.

What do you see when you look at those things that God called you to accomplish and receive? What do you see and how do you speak about what God has shown you? Do you believe that God will allow you to possess the land of milk and honey, even if there are giants in the land? He will make a way out of what appears to have no way out. He will allow you to possess the land even though your credit scores are low. He will give you a new job, even though there is an inside candidate. God will do whatever He said He will do. If God calls it, He will bring it to pass. Keep your eyes and heart on Jesus. You are well able to possess all that God has promised you.

> *You are well able to possess all that God has promised you.*

Faith Affirmation: *I am well able to possess the land in the name of Jesus.*

Prayer: Lord, I thank You for another day to report the goodness of Jesus Christ (Ps. 118:24). "[You] are great. . . Honor and majesty are before [You]: strength and beauty are in [Your] sanctuary" (Ps. 96:4, 6). O Lord, You are "my strength, and my redeemer" (Ps. 19:14). You are "full of compassion, and gracious, long suffering, and plenteous in mercy and truth" (Ps. 86:15). In the name of Jesus, I will possess the land. I am well able to overcome any situation by trusting in You.

Dear God Letter: Talk to God about your day. Remember to move forward at once to possess your tomorrow and to overcome the giants. **What is your report?**

Dear God,

WHAT DO YOU SEE?

And the God said, Let us make man in our image, after our likeness . . .
(Gen. 1:26).

There is a children's story written by Bill Martin titled *Brown Bear, Brown Bear, What Do You See?* The book helps children learn their colors and the names of different animals in a fun way. The reader is asked to describe what he/she sees. For example, you turn the page and say, "I see a blue horse looking at me or a purple cat looking at me and so on and so on." I believe the Lord is asking each one of us what do we see when we look at ourselves and our life circumstances. When you look in the mirror are you able to say, I see a beautiful child of God looking at me? I see the faith and love of God all over me. I see all that God has called me to be looking at me. I see Jesus looking at me. It is important that you see who God has called you to be.

When you are full of God's joy, take a mental snapshot and a real live snapshot of yourself and put that picture in a place where you and others can see it. Tell the story about the picture and your joy. When you find yourself working hard on a project, make a mental imprint and spiritual note, and snap a picture. As folks spend time looking at your picture, talk to them about what was going on at that time and what you see and still feel. You have got to find ways to hold on to what you see. The more you see yourself walking in God's calling, the more you can experience the power of the Holy Spirit.

Depression, defeat, hopelessness, and fear are not a part of how God sees you or your circumstance. If you look in the mirror and see those things that are not of God, then speak to that image in Jesus' Name and challenge yourself to see what God sees –love, joy, victory, hope, courage, and power. Speak Out! I am the love of God. I am full of God's hope and strength. I am more than a conqueror through Christ Jesus. I am strong and shielded by the favor of the Lord. I am because I AM lives within me.

77

Each day press to see you like Jesus sees you. I see God's favor looking at me. In fact, it's all over me. I see that I can do all things through Christ who strengthens me (Phil. 4:13). I see God's glory. I see the impossible made possible through Christ Jesus. I see myself feeding the hungry. I see myself preaching the Word of God. I see myself singing and people being saved. I see myself teaching and people being blessed and receiving Christ. I see myself walking in my calling.

I hope you see yourself as God sees you. I hope you see yourself doing God's will in the name of Jesus. I encourage you to be honest with yourself about what you see. I ask you to see yourself moving in your calling and releasing the Holy Spirit to bring you into His

> *I see a beautiful child of God looking at me.*

perfect way (Ps.18:30). "Faithful is He that calleth you, who also will do it" (1 Thess. 5:24). I encourage you to hold on to the goodness of God; its medicine for the heart and a light unto your path. I encourage you to hold onto what God sees; a child made in His likeness and image and filled with Him.

Faith Affirmation: *I see the goodness of God in me.*

Prayer: Lord I thank You for this day (Ps. 118:24). You are "my strength and my redeemer" (Ps. 19:14). I see that "I am fearfully and wonderfully made" by You (Ps. 139:14). It is because of You that I live, breathe, and have my existence (Acts 17:28). Lord, I thank You for opening my spiritual eyes so that I can see You in my life and inside of me (1 Cor. 3:16). "How excellent is [Your] name in all the earth!" (Ps. 8:1).

Dear God Letter: Talk to God about your day. Remember you are the apple of God's eye, fearfully and wonderfully made by Him and shielded by His favor. **What do you see?**

Dear God,

Date:
Day #:

GOD'S BLESSINGS AND GOOD PLEASURE

For it is God which worketh in you both to will and to do of His good pleasure (Phil. 2:13).

We are God's workmanship and have been created with a divine purpose. On our journey to reach our purpose, there will be many opportunities, circumstances, and obstacles that require us to use our gifts, skills, and possessions to do God's will and good pleasure. We must trust God to use and bless us, as we strive toward our divine purpose in the name of Jesus.

God blessed:
- ♥ David with a faith testimony, a sling shot, and 5 stones to defeat Goliath, the giant Philistine (1 Sam. 17).
- ♥ Esther with beauty and courage to go in the presence of the King for "such a time as this" on behalf of the Jews (Est. 5).
- ♥ Naomi with her daughter-in-law Ruth's faithfulness, companionship, and desire to take care of her mother-in-law, and belief in her God (Ruth 1-4).
- ♥ Ruth with a commitment to her mother-in-law, a marriage to a wealthy man, Boaz, and the birth of Obed, the father of Jesse, who is the father of David (Ruth 4:17).
- ♥ Samson with the jawbone of an ass to slay a thousand Philistines (Judg. 15:14-17).
- ♥ Hananiah, Azariah, and Mishael with unadulterated faith that led to a fourth man being in the burning fiery furnace with them, whose form was like the Son of God (Dan. 3).
- ♥ Mary with an ointment that she poured on Jesus' holy feet and dried them with her hair as she worshiped Him (Jn. 12:3).

♥ Paul with intelligence, faith, and an unrelenting commitment and zeal that allowed him to preach the gospel of Jesus Christ to high priests, kings, and masses of believers and unbelievers (Acts 9-28).
♥ Jeremiah with fire shut up in his bones that led him to do God's will (Jer. 20:9).

As Christians, God has blessed us, and He has filled us with Himself, the Holy Spirit, who chooses and anoints our gifts and talents, reveals the snares of life, tears down strongholds, and guides us on an unimaginable journey that leads us to fulfill His will, good pleasures, and our divine purpose. What a blessing!

Faith Affirmation: *I will allow God to use whatever He chooses.*

Prayer: Lord, I thank You for today (Ps. 118:24), another day to delight in doing Your will (Ps. 37:3-4). You created the heavens and earth (Gen. 1:1) and all that is within it, which includes me (Ps. 24:1). You work in me, and You do the unimaginable in my life. I am blessed by You, and I will do Your will and good pleasure (Phil. 2:13). I love You, Lord.

Dear God Letter: Talk to God about your day. Remember God works in you to do His will and **His good pleasure**.

Dear God,

Date:
Day #:

JOY COMETH

For His anger endureth but a moment; in His favor is life: weeping may endure for a night, but joy cometh in the morning (Ps. 30:5).

Life seems to be a journey full of ups and downs, trials and tribulations, peace and strife, joy and sadness, hardships and victories, disappointments and satisfactions, and good and evil. Depending on the severity of the matter, your place in life, and/or your attitude and walk with God, a hardship can cause you to weep. If we do not allow the Holy Spirit to minister to our hearts, the weeping can lead to discouragement, which leads to doubt; which leads to disappointment, which leads to feelings of helplessness, hopelessness or despair; which leads to defeat.

Whatever the situation, you must hold on to the Lord. Whatever the situation, cry out to the Lord and tell Him all about it (Ps. 27:7). Don't hold it in and try to handle it by yourself; only God has the answer. Hold on to God's unchanging hand. You have to know that you know – that you know, that in God's favor there is life. Your weeping (hurt, despair, discouragement, and hopelessness) endures for only a night – only the time it takes for you to return to God's light and embrace His love for you. Joy comes in the morning –in the moment that you trust God,

> *Joy comes in the morning.*

surrender your situation to Him, and call on the name of Jesus. God loves you. Oh, how He loves you. He wants you to know that He is with you through it all, and no matter the circumstance cry out to Him and allow His love for you and gift of eternal life to bring you joy.

Faith Affirmation: *Lord, I claim Your joy in my moment.*

Prayer: Father, I thank You for another day (Ps. 118:24) to praise You with my whole heart (Ps. 9:1). I accept Your joy today. I know that Your joy is my strength (Neh. 8:10). I thank You for wiping away my tears and filling me with Your joy. You are "my strength and my shield; my heart trusted in [You], and I am helped: therefore my heart greatly rejoiceth; and with my song will I praise [You]" (Ps. 28:7).

Dear God Letter: Talk to God about your day. Remember **joy comes in the morning** and to tell God how much you appreciate His blessings.

Dear God,

THE BLESSINGS OF OBEDIENCE

*And Simon answering said unto Him, Master, we have toiled all the night,
and have taken nothing: nevertheless at thy word I will let down the net
(Lk. 5:5).*

Peter and the disciples were skilled fishermen who had cast their nets
out into the waters hoping to catch an abundance of fish. But their long
hours in the waters had not yielded them the big catch of the day. So, they
gave up on trying and returned to the shore to wash their fishing nets and
called it a night. I'm sure they were tired and feeling somewhat discouraged.
They had depended on their fishermen skills to supply their needs, but on
this day there were no fish to be caught. How disappointing.

Jesus arrived on the shore and stepped into the ship where the men were
washing their nets and wrapping up for the evening. He took the time to
speak to the disciples and from the boat taught the people. After teaching
the people, Jesus asked Simon to go out into the deep water and let down
the fishing net. Simon responded, "Master, we have toiled all the night, and
have taken nothing: **nevertheless at thy word** I will let down the net" (Lk.
5:5). I will let down the net; even though I know that there were no fish out
there earlier tonight, I will be obedient to Your request. You are all knowing!
Simon and the men did as Jesus requested, and they caught an enormous
amount of fish, so much that their nets began to break (Lk. 5:6). The boat
also began to sink because of the weight of the fish, and Peter had to call for
help. The disciples' obedience led to a blessing filled with more than they
could understand or comprehend.

The men were totally astonished at the amount of fish they had caught.
They were fishermen and knew their trade well, yet, they had never caught
that amount of fish. Simon recognized that because of Jesus they had caught
such an abundance of fish. Simon fell at the feet of Jesus acknowledging the
Holy One. Jesus spoke to Simon and said, "Fear not; from henceforth thou
shall catch men" (Lk. 5:10).

We all have gifts and talents that God created at our very existence and has honed them through our life experiences. Are you using your gifts to meet your day-to-day needs? Are you disappointed because you are not reaping what you expected or anticipated? God has given you these gifts and talents and requires that you use them for the building of His kingdom. Listen, as God tells you where to launch your net (gifts, skills, ideas, etc.) and receive your blessings. I know that you have let it down on many different occasions and situations, but this time let it down when and where God tells you to.

You may be saying "Lord, I've done all I can to repair my marriage." "I have tried to speak into my friend's life but to no avail; he is still depressed." "I have reached out to people through my ministry, but my church isn't growing. The people just will not hearken unto Your Word." "I'm tired and disappointed. I'm washing my hands of this situation. I'll try another time."

> *Nevertheless, at thy word, Lord.*

God is saying, "Trust me and lower your net where I tell You to lower it. Be obedient to my voice and request. It is I who will repair, heal, and give you abundance. It is I who will bless you and my people." You must trust God and respond to where He tells you to cast your net. He will anoint your gifts and talents so that you are blessed and positioned to bless others. You have been created for God's glory (Isa. 43:7).

Faith Affirmation: *Nevertheless at thy word. . . .*

Prayer: Lord, I thank You for another day (Ps. 118:24) to honor You through my obedience. You are great and the King of my life and over all the earth (Ps. 47:2). I pray to continue to hear Your voice and to be obedient to Your Word. I pray to move even when it doesn't make sense to me.

Dear God Letter: Talk to God about your day. Remember at God's word to let down your net, and you will receive **the blessings of your obedience**.

Dear God,

WHATSOEVER STATE BE CONTENT

Not that I speak in respect of want: for I have learned, in whatsoever state I am, therewith to be content (Phil. 4:11). . . . I can do all things through Christ which strengtheneth me (Phil. 4:13).

Content: happy, satisfied, pleased, and comfortable

In his letter to the Philippi church, Paul shares his continued faith and commitment to God with the members. He reminds the Christians that the Lord is at hand (Phil. 4:5). God is near unto them and will return for His people. Paul tells the Christians to "be careful for nothing – [don't worry or be anxious]; but in everything by prayer and supplication with thanksgiving let their requests be made known unto God" (Phil. 4:6). As he wraps up his letter, he tells them to think on whatsoever things are true, honest, just, pure, lovely, and of good report (Phil. 4:8).

Paul is basically writing the recipe for contentment. As a servant of Christ, who had been ridiculed, beaten and was currently in prison, he had grown to be content in all circumstances. His contentment lay in his ability to trust in the Lord who provided him strength in all situations. In keeping his heart and mind focused on Jesus, Paul had learned to rejoice in the Lord in any circumstance. He learned to be content in whatsoever state, whether abased or abound; with or without. He knew that no matter the circumstances he "[could] do all things through Christ which [strengthens] him" (Phil. 4:13). He had committed to keeping his heart and mind on the love, might, and power of Jesus Christ.

It was God who guarded and directed his path (Prov. 3:5-6). It was God who ordered his footsteps (Ps. 37:23). It was God who would be "with [him] always, even unto the end of the world" (Matt. 28:20). It was God who would show him how to adapt to every life situation. It was God who was in control of his life. It was God whom he would be with upon his departure from this earth. Paul writes, "For me to live is Christ, and to die is gain" (Phil. 1:21). Paul was "sold out" to Jesus. His total trust and faith in God allowed him to be content in all things and rejoice. Follow Paul's contentment recipe and you too can be content in whatsoever state or situation you find yourself in life.

Faith Affirmation: *I will be content in the Lord.*

Prayer: Lord, I thank You for today (Ps. 118:24). You are great and I will exalt Your name forever (Ps. 118:28). It is in You that I live, breathe and have my existence (Acts 17:28). You order my footsteps and make the crooked places straight (Isa. 45:2). I strive to rest in You and to be content in all situations. "I can do all things through Christ which strengthens me" (Phil. 4:13).

Dear God Letter: Talk to God about your day. Remember **whatsoever state you are in to be content** in the name of Jesus.

Dear God,

Date:
Day #:

I PRAISE AND THANK YOU

It is a good thing to give thanks unto the LORD, and to sing praises unto thy name, O Most High (Ps. 92:1).

Lord, I praise You (Ps. 71:14).
I will exalt Your holy name (Ps. 29:2).
I will praise You all day long and for the rest of my life (Ps. 86:12).
I will sing praises to You for evermore (Ps. 104:33).
I will praise You for Your mighty acts (Jer. 33:3).
I will praise You from the depths of my soul (Ps. 103:1).

You are the creator of the heavens and earth (Ps. 24:1).
You are mighty and great (Ps. 24:8).
"How excellent is [Your] name in all the earth!" (Ps. 8:1).
You are beyond what I can conceive or comprehend (Isa. 55:8-9).
Your mercy is new every morning and endures forever (Lam. 3:23).
You are God and there is none like You (Isa. 45:5).
You are my Father (Eph. 4:6).

Lord, I thank You (Eph. 5:20).
I thank You for creating me and providing me with a divine purpose (Isa. 43:7).
I thank You for giving me wings like eagles so that I can soar high (Isa. 40:31).
I thank You for calling me to do greater things in the name of Jesus (Jn. 14:12).
I thank You for hearing my prayers and answering them (Isa. 65:24).
I thank You for correcting me out of Your love for me (2 Tim. 3:16).
I thank You for Your grace and mercy (Ps. 84:11).
I thank You for daily loading me with Your benefits (Ps. 68:19).
I thank You for Your favor in my life (Ps. 5:12).

I thank You for Your gift of salvation (Eph. 2:8-9).
I thank You for guiding me into Your perfect will for my life (Ps. 18:32).
I thank You for everything that You have done and will continue to do
(1 Thess. 5:24).
I thank You for giving me a heart filled with praise and joy (Phil. 4:4).
I thank You for loving me (Jn. 3:16; Jer. 31:3)!

I thank and praise You
I thank and praise You for _____
I thank and praise You for _____
I thank and praise You for _____
With my whole heart, I thank and praise You!

Faith Affirmation: *I will forever praise and thank the Lord.*

Prayer: Lord, I thank You for another day to praise and worship You (Ps. 118:24). I will praise You O, Lord and "give thanks unto [You]; for [You] are good: for Your mercy endureth forever" (Ps. 106:1). "O God, my heart is fixed; I will sing and give [You] praise" (Ps. 108:1). "From the rising of the sun unto the going down of the same [Your] name is to be praised" (Ps. 113:3).

Dear God Letter: Talk to God about your day. Remember **to praise and thank God**. It's a good thing to give God thanks; to sing praises to Him and to tell God how much you love Him.

Dear God,

TURN FLIPS

We are troubled on every side, yet not distressed, we are perplexed,
but not in despair; persecuted, but not forsaken; cast down, but not
destroyed; always bearing about in the body the dying of the Lord Jesus,
that the life also of Jesus might be made manifest in our body
(2 Cor. 4:8-10).

A friend called me to tell me about one of her dreams. My friend, her 3 year old son and I were fighting in a war. All of a sudden, she looked around and the enemy had surrounded and captured us and others who were fighting.

The soldiers took all of the prisoners-of-war and placed them in a line. She began frantically looking for her young son and me. She says that she doesn't know what happened to me. I'd like to think that I escaped. Well anyway, she continued to look around in hopes of locating her son. At the end of the line, she spotted her son. He didn't have a worried or concerned look on his face. He was not crying. She gave out a sigh of relief. In fact, he was doing something that did not match this dangerous situation. While standing in the line, he was turning flips. How could this be – didn't he realize they were in a dangerous predicament.

Her son's behavior reminded me that when the going gets tough and the situation feels overwhelming, just do something out of the ordinary —start turning flips. Don't allow the situation to dictate your behavior. Clear your mind and turn a flip, a cartwheel, swing on the monkey bars, hit a home run, spin, and shoot your jumper.

Clear your mind and turn a flip.

Basically, think on those things that are good, right and just (Phil. 4:8). Meditate on God and all that He has done and will do. Take the time to create a place of praise and worship. Yes, the storm may continue to rage but it won't consume you.

Remember that God the Holy Spirit resides within you (1 Cor. 6:19). God has anointed you. Have faith in the power and might of the Lord. Your faith in God will change your sadness to joy; confusion to peace, discouragement to encouragement, defeat to victory. Hey, take a deep breath, activate your faith in God and turn a flip. "If at first you don't succeed, try, try again."

Faith Affirmation: *Lord, I am turning flips in the name of Jesus.*

Prayer: Lord, I thank You for this day (Ps. 118:24) and the opportunity to turn a flip. You are awesome and worthy to be praised. Lord, You are "my light and my salvation; whom shall I fear?" (Ps. 27:1). You are "the strength of my life; of whom shall I be afraid?" (Ps. 27:1). When You said, "Seek ye my face; my heart said unto [You], thy face, LORD, will I seek" (Ps. 27:8). "In thee, O LORD, do I put my trust. . . deliver me in thy righteousness" (Ps. 31:1).

Dear God Letter: Talk to God about your day. Remember your confidence is in God. Ask according to His will **and turn some flips** while you wait on His answer.

Dear God,

THE LORD IS ON MY SIDE

The LORD is on my side; I will not fear: what can man do unto me?
(Ps. 118:6)

D avid, the adolescent Shepherd boy, was confident in the Lord and His ability to deliver Goliath into his hands. This defeat would once again show God's awesome power and remind the Israelites and Philistines that God is Lord. He did not fear, but the men of the armies of the living God feared and fled from Goliath (1 Sam. 17:24). David knew without a doubt that Goliath, the uncircumcised champion Philistine, was just a man and no match for God. He had a heart of faith, trust, and victory. God was "the Lord strong and mighty, the Lord mighty in battle" (Ps. 24:8).

David had established that the Lord was his light and salvation; he need not fear. The Lord was the strength of his life; he need not be afraid (Ps. 27:1). Though Goliath intended to defeat the armies of the living God, the Lord intended that the Philistines would be defeated, and His name would be exalted that all the earth would know that there is a God in Israel (1 Sam. 17:46). David proclaimed for all to hear, "The LORD is on my side; I will not fear; for what can man do unto me?" (Ps. 118:6). He knew his enemies could do nothing unto him.

"The Lord is on [your] side" (Ps. 118:6). You know the One who has all power in His hands and dwells within you (1 Cor. 3:16). You need not fear because people cannot do anything unto you (Ps. 118:6). You do not have to fear anyone. You don't have to fear what others say about you; God has already called and named you. You don't have to fear your future. God orders the steps of the righteous.

> *The Lord is on your side, fear thou not.*

You don't have to fear anything, for God is "with you always, even until the end of the world" (Matt. 28:20).

Faith Affirmation: *The Lord is on my side.*

Prayer: Lord, I thank You for another day to stand with confidence in the name of Jesus. Though my enemies – fear, failure, deception, regret, mistrust, depression – should encamp against me, I will remain confident that You will protect me and deliver me (Ps. 27:2-3), and I will give You the praise and glory due Your name (Ps. 29:2). I will forever praise You (Ps. 150). I thank You for being on my side.

Dear God Letter: Talk to God about your day. Remember there is no need to fear what man can do to you. **The Lord is on your side.**

Dear God,

WHAT'S IN A DELAY?

And the Philistine drew near morning and evening, and presented himself forty days (1 Sam. 17:16).

Goliath, the Philistine warrior and enemy of the Israelites, presented himself forty days. In those forty days, he came to the valley and shouted across to the armies of Israel what he planned to do to them. Each day he presented himself to the armies of Israel and the men trembled with fear. They were afraid because Goliath was a giant and a champion warrior. His height, stature, and his warrior history preceded him (1 Sam. 17:4). Goliath brought with him a history of fighting and a long track record of victories.

Each time Goliath presented himself to the men of Israel, they allowed him to get into their minds and produce fear. He used these forty days to intimidate them and incite fear. However, God used the 40 days to bring forth His blessing. Unbeknownst to David and the Israelite army, God was smack dab in the middle of this 40-day delay. You ask, "How so?"

David would be asked by his father to take provisions to his brothers who had gone to battle with Saul against the Philistines. He also was to bring a report back to his father regarding his brothers and the status of the battle. Basically, he was just going to check on his brothers and return home with a report. However, when he entered the Israel army camp, he heard the Philistine of Gath, Goliath, challenging the armies of the living God. He also saw how God's men fled. David inquired with the men, "What shall be done to the man that killeth this Philistine, and taketh away the reproach from Israel?" (1 Sam. 17:26). David also wanted to know "Who is this uncircumcised Philistine, that he should defy the armies of the living God?" (1 Sam. 17:26).

A forty-day delay allowed God to send His blessing, David. David would step onto the battlefield and run to the battle line with the Lord of

Hosts. He would defeat Goliath with a stone from his sling and the power and might of God. David and the men were victorious because God had fought this battle (1 Sam. 17:47). In the delay, God manifested His plan and His glory. So, what's in your delay? The same thing that was in this forty-day delay — God's blessings. Whatever your situation don't lose heart, God is working out His plan and preparing to present His blessing. Stay encouraged!

> *There is a blessing in a delay.*

Faith Affirmation: *God is in my delay!*

Prayer: Lord, I praise You, and I will "give unto [You] the glory due [Your] name (Ps. 29:2). "How excellent is [Your] name in all [the] earth!" (Ps. 8:1). Your Word says, "Even the youths shall faint and be weary, and the young men shall utterly fall: But they that wait upon the Lord shall renew their strength; they shall mount up with wings as eagles; they shall run, and not be weary; and they shall walk, and not faint" (Isa. 40:30-31). I will wait on You Lord. You are my strength and protection.

Dear God Letter: Talk to God about your day. **What's in a delay?** There is a blessing in your delay.

Dear God,

GOD YOU ARE . . .

And Moses said unto God. . .and [the children of Israel] shall say to me, What is His name? What shall I say unto them? And God said unto Moses, I AM THAT I AM. . .I AM hath sent me unto you (Ex. 3:13-14).

GOD YOU ARE:

Adored
Alive
All-powerful
Alpha
Amazing
Astounding
Awesome
Beloved
Benevolent
Bold
Boundless
Breathtaking
Compassionate
Complete
Consistent
Courageous
Deliberate
Dependable
Divine
Endless
Everlasting
Everything
Excellent

Exceptional
Exemplary
Faithful
Fantastic
Faultless
Forever
Forgiving
Generous
Gentle
GOD
Good
Great
Grace
Happiness
Holy
Honorable
Hope
Incredible
Indescribable
Incomparable
Invincible
I AM THAT I AM
Jehovah

Joy

Just

Kind

King of kings

Life

Living Water

LORD

Love

Magnificent

Majestic

Marvelous

Mercy

Mighty

Mind-blowing

Mmm Good

Never-ending

Nourishment

Omega

Omnipotent

Omnipresent

Omniscient

Off The Hook

Out of this World

Outstanding

Passionate

Patient

Peace

Perfect

Powerful

Praiseworthy

Quintessential

Redemption

Regal

Reliable

Remarkable

Righteous

Royalty

Spirit

Steadfast

Supreme

Superb

Stupendous

Sweet

Tender

Terrific

Tremendous

Trustworthy

Truth

Ubiquitous

Unchangeable

Uncontainable

Undefeated

Unfaltering

Unmatched

Unstoppable

Unwavering

Vibrant

Victorious

Warm

Wise

Wonderful

Worthy

"X"traordinary

Yeshua

Yahweh

Zealous

Zumdiliumpcious

(Zum-dill-e-ump-shus)

God, there is no limit to You or words to truly describe who You are, because You are God.

Faith Affirmation: *God, You are everything to me.*

Prayer: Lord, I thank You for another day to glorify Your name and to rejoice (Ps. 118:24). You are an awesome God. Lord, You reign over the heavens and earth (Ps. 97). You are God and "there is no God beside [You]" (Isa. 45:5). You are I AM THAT I AM (Ex. 3:14). I will bow down and worship You (Ps. 95:6). You exceed everything I think or could imagine.

Dear God Letter: Talk to God about your day. Remember **who God is**.

Dear God,

STAND GUARD

Keep thy heart with all diligence; for out of it are the issues of life
(Prov. 4:23).

The Word says that we should "keep [or guard our] heart with all diligence; for out of it are the issues of life" (Prov. 4:23). Most people lock up or guard things that they perceive to be of value. The more valuable, the more effort spent to guard it. We have guards at banks, apartment buildings, schools, stores, work sites and so on. We place alarms on our cars, houses, and businesses. We do all of this in an attempt to guard our worldly possessions.

We should also guard our heart and mind through the power of the Holy Spirit. "[Satan] come[s] not, but for to steal, and to kill, and to destroy" (Jn. 10:10) our heart, mind, and life. God came that we would have life –joy, hope, love, peace, power, perseverance —and have life more abundantly (Jn. 10:10). What have you put in place to guard your heart? What have you put in place to guard your thoughts and attitude? God has given you a 24-hour guard service. He has filled you with himself, the Holy Spirit (1 Cor. 3:16) and charged His angels to watch over you (Ps. 91:11).

Have you opened your heart and mind to the Holy Spirit, your 24-hour guard? Have you surrendered your life and your life situations to God? The peace of God will guard your heart and mind. Take time to read and meditate on the Word of God. Allow His living Word to rest and minister to your heart; for out of your heart comes the issues of life

> *Guard your heart and mind through the power of the Holy Spirit.*

(Prov. 4:23). Take time to praise and worship, God the Father, the Son, and the Holy Spirit. Challenge yourself to think on those thoughts that are right, good, and just (Phil. 4:8). Think on those thoughts that are pleasing unto the Lord. Be diligent and do those things that will keep your heart and mind on the goodness, power, love, and authority of Jesus Christ, no matter the situation.

Do those things that are good medicine for the heart and out of your heart shall flow joy, peace, hope, trust, compassion, love, and many other attributes of God. Daily guard your heart by keeping your mind on God and allowing Him to direct your path (Prov. 3:5-6; 16:9).

Faith Affirmation: *I will guard my heart through the power of the Holy Spirit.*

Prayer: Lord, I thank You that "this is the day which [You] hath made; [I] will rejoice and be glad in it" (Ps. 118:24). I will guard my heart with Your goodness, peace, joy, power, hope, and love. I will pray without ceasing (1 Thess. 5:17). I will listen for Your voice and be obedient to Your Word and direction (Jn. 10:4). I will strive for a righteous heart, a heart that is acceptable unto You.

Dear God Letter: Talk to God about your day. Remember to call on the Holy Spirit; He gives you strength to **stand guard over your heart** in the name of Jesus.

Dear God,

Date:
Day #:

HE'S CLOSER THAN YOU THINK

I am with you always, even unto the end of the world (Matt. 28:20).

Good morning. God is at the center of your morning; have you paused to say "good morning?" If you haven't yet, take 5 minutes and give Him the praise and honor that He deserves (Ps. 29:2). Take five minutes to sit with God so that He may start your day.

Good afternoon. God is at the center of your afternoon, have you checked in with Him yet. Oh, I know you may have said "good morning," but have you said good afternoon? Have you asked God to direct your afternoon? Have you asked God to take a look at your heart and guide you through His day? Take five minutes out of your afternoon and talk with God. He wants to hear from you, and He wants to talk with you.

Oh, it's evening time and you're probably preparing for bed. God is at the center of your evening. You still have time to praise Him and thank Him for His day. You have time to talk to God about your day. You can pour your heart out before God. Take five minutes and talk to God. He loves to hear from you. He knows that the more you talk to Him, the more you experience His love, mercy, grace, and awesome power. God also knows that the more you talk to Him and He talks to you, the more you will experience His love, favor, joy, peace, and presence – a closer walk and relationship with Him.

With time, your five minutes with the Father will become 10 minutes, then 15 minutes, and on and on. With each breath, you will acknowledge God as the center of your life. A songwriter wrote, "Jesus [is] at the center of it all. Nothing else matters, nothing in this world will do. Jesus you're the center, and everything revolves around you."

> *God wants to hear from you.*

The more you spend time with God, the more you think about Him and hear his loving voice (Jn. 10:4). God will order your footsteps (Ps. 37:23) and show you the way to your divine calling. Believe me, the time that you spend with God will be life changing. You will never be the same.

Faith Affirmation: *Lord, I will spend time with You.*

Prayer: Lord, I thank You for another day to walk and talk with You (Ps. 118:24). "I will bless [You] at all times: [Your] praise shall continually be in my mouth" (Ps. 34:1). "For thou art my hope, O Lord GOD: thou art my trust from my youth" (Ps. 71:5). Lord, You are God. You are "full of compassion, and gracious, long suffering, and plenteous in mercy and truth" (Ps. 86:15). I thank You for talking to me, listening to me, answering my call, and most of all, I thank You for loving me. I love You, Lord.

Dear God Letter: Talk to God about your day. Remember that **He's closer than you think**.

Dear God,

FULLY ARMED

When a strong man armed keepeth his palace, his goods are in peace:
But when a stronger than he shall come upon him, and overcome him, he
taketh from him all his armour wherein he trusted, and divideth
his spoils (Lk. 11:21-22).

O ften times, when we are under attack we don't put on our God-given armor. We don't even realize we need our armor. We run because we fear our situation. We begin to fight in the flesh with our earthly ways. We start using our untamed tongue to fight, our hands and feet to hurt and our silence to condemn. We sit idle and take the blows of the attack. We also try breathing, meditation, and avoidance strategies hoping the attack will end. In short, we activate the tools of the flesh, not the armor of God. We are now susceptible to Satan overpowering us, taking our possessions and dividing them up. The Word is clear and specific, "Wherefore take unto you the whole armor of God, that ye may be able to withstand in the evil day, and having done all, to stand. Stand . . ." (Eph. 6:13-14). Many of us can and will quote Eph. 6:13, but is it in your heart? Do you truly wear the spiritual garment needed for each and every day? Selah (pause)

I'm sure most of us have learned how to put on the earthly/carnal garments (clothing, gossip, fear, disappointment, anguish, hurt, pain, worry, conflict, envy, strife, etc.) but do you know how to put on God's spiritual armor? God requires that we put on His spiritual armor, which withstands in all situations. What type of armor have you trusted in? Does your current armor overpower the attack of someone stronger, and does it prevent the dividing up of your spoils? Does it prevent the division of your family, marriage, finances, thoughts, peace, joy, and relationship with God the Father, God the Son and God the Holy Spirit? Are your possessions safe? They are only safe if you have put on the full armor of God. Therefore, take the time to put on God's armor; it is your defense against the enemy.

Faith Affirmation: *I have put on the armor of God and will fight in the name of Jesus.*

Prayer: Lord, I thank You for another day (Ps. 118:24) and opportunity to put on Your armor. "For thou art great, and doest wondrous things: thou art God alone" (Ps. 86:10). "I will praise thee, O Lord my God, with all my heart: and I will glorify [Your] name for evermore" (Ps. 86:12). I thank You for providing me with the whole armor of God so that I may stand and be victorious in these evil days (Eph. 6:13). I thank You that I am able to stand. You are my defense and the rock of my refuge (Ps. 94:22).

Dear God Letter: Talk to God about your day. Remember to stay **fully armed** and to guard your temple.

Dear God,

Date:
Day #:

YOUR WILL OR GOD'S WILL?

I delight to do thy will, O my God: yea, thy law is within my heart (Ps. 40:8).

L et your heart and mind stay focused on doing God's will, not your will. It is God's will that you live in His perfect peace (Isa. 26:3). Your will leads you down the path of disobedience and bondage, which leads to personal and spiritual destruction.

Jesus came to fulfill the will of his Father (Jn. 6:38) and now through the Holy Spirit that lives within you, you are called to fulfill the will of the Father and the Son. You are called to do those things that are pleasing unto the Lord, those things that lead you to the throne of the Father. Let your spirit delight to do the will of the Father which is your heartfelt response to His love, mercy, and grace.

Your will:
- ♥ Determines if your words defile your body (Matt. 15: 17-20) – your choice.
- ♥ Determines if you will do God's good pleasure (Phil. 2:13) – your choice.
- ♥ Determines if your heart holds evil thoughts (Matt. 15:18-19) – your choice.
- ♥ Determines if you sit in the seat of the scornful (Ps. 1:1-2) – your choice.
- ♥ Determines if you judge lest you be judged by God (Matt. 7:1-2) – your choice.
- ♥ Determines if you murmur or dispute (Phil. 2: 14) – your choice.
- ♥ Determines if your soul will prosper (3 Jn. 1:2) – your choice
- ♥ Determines if discretion will lead you in the right way (Isa. 28:21-26) – your choice.

109

- ♥ Determines if you will do things the LORD hates (Prov. 6:16-19) – your choice.
- ♥ Determines if you will dwell in God's love (1 Jn. 4:8, 11, 16) – your choice.
- ♥ Determines if you will practice sin or habitually live in sin (1 Jn. 3:1-7) – your choice.
- ♥ Determines if patience is persevering through problems, trials, and tribulations (Col. 1:3-13) – your choice.
- ♥ Determines if you will live in liberty (Gal. 5:1) – your choice
- ♥ Determines if you walk in Christ Jesus the Lord (Col. 2:6-7) – your choice.

God's Will has already predetermined your purpose. Your will makes the choices that bring your purpose to fruition. **God's Will** will not overpower your choice. But **God's Will** will be done. The amount of time it takes is determined by your choices. God the Holy Spirit works in you, so your ministry and service will succeed. It is God's desire that you do His good pleasure (Phil. 2:13). As Jesus sits on the right hand of the Father interceding for you (Rom. 8:34), the Comforter, God the Holy Spirit, is producing in you a desire, a need, and a longing to do **His Will**.

Faith Affirmation: *I delight to do God's will.*

Prayer: Lord, I thank You for today (Ps. 118:24). "Thou art my God, and I will praise thee: thou art my God, I will exalt thee" (Ps. 118:28). I worship and adore You. I will continue to hide Your Word in my heart (Ps. 119:11). Lord, "I delight to do Your will" (Ps. 40:8) and to be pleasing unto You (Prov. 16:7). I love You.

Dear God Letter: Talk to God about your day. Remember to **delight to do His will** and to hide His Word in your heart.

Dear God,

THIS DAY

This day will the Lord deliver thee into mine hand . . . (1 Sam. 17:46).

G oliath, the Philistine giant and skilled warrior, came out to the battlefield to taunt the men of the armies of Israel and had been quite
successful. He challenged the men of Israel to send out a man to fight him.
Whoever won the battle would rule the other. Goliath and the Philistine
armies knew that none of the men of Israel would defeat Goliath. I'm sure
the Philistines were already rejoicing and celebrating their victory.

Goliath came out on the final day ready to kill his opponent, David,
the adolescent shepherd boy, who declared he would kill Goliath. Goliath
"saw David [and] he disdained him" (1 Sam. 17:42). Goliath became angry
and insulted because the armies of Israel sent David, a young boy, who was
not a warrior, nor was he dressed for battle.
Goliath cursed David by the gods of the
Philistines. He also told David that he would
kill him and give his "flesh unto the fowls of
the air and to the beasts of the field" (1 Sam.
17:44). David stood strong and replied . . . "I
come to thee in the name of the Lord of hosts,
the God of the armies of Israel, whom thou have defied. This day the Lord
will deliver thee into mine hand; and I will smite thee, and take thine head
from thee. . ." (1 Sam. 17:45-46).

This day the Lord will deliver you.

As Christians, we are also taunted by giants (depression, anxiety, heart-
ache, low self-esteem, health concerns, regret, fear, disappointment, etc.).
Giants that attempt to destroy us. They seem to get bigger and bigger each
day, week, month, and year. Giants that seek to incite fear, kill our hopes and
dreams, keep us off balance, and take away our peace and joy. Giants that
come to kill, steal, and destroy (Jn. 10:10). But remember, God has given
us the power to defeat the giants in the name of Jesus. We must believe
in our hearts, at the core of our being, that God is more powerful than we

113

can ever imagine. We must speak forth God's Word with an unshakeable faith and confidence. God's Word will go forth and it will destroy the giant. His "[Word] shall not return unto [Him] void, but it shall accomplish that which [He] please[s], and it shall prosper in the things whereto [He] sent it" (Isa. 55:11). Make your declaration to your giant today, "This day the Lord will deliver thee into mine hand . . . for the battle is the Lord's" (1 Sam. 17:46-47).

Faith Affirmation: *This day God will deliver _____ into my hands.*

Prayer: Lord, I thank You for this day (Ps. 118:24). You are gracious, righteous, mighty and merciful (Ps. 116:5). I will bless and praise You forever (Ps. 115:18). I expect a victory for no other reason than You are God, and a right now God at that! "The battle is [Yours]" (1 Sam. 17:47).

Dear God Letter: Talk to God about your day. Remember the giants of **this day** have been delivered into your hands in the name of Jesus, and you reign in victory.

Dear God,

SHUT UP IN MY BONES

Then I said, I will not make mention of Him, nor speak any more in His name. But His word was in mine heart as a burning fire shut up in my bones, and I was weary and forbearing, and I could not stay (Jer. 20:9).

I believe that everyone has a great calling on their life. In order to reach our calling, we must allow God to shape us. He is the potter and we are the clay (Isa. 64:8). It is He who created us for greatness and to give Him glory (Isa. 43:7). It is He who created us and has called us to fulfill our divine purpose in life. God wants to guide us into greater works than His son, Jesus Christ (Jn. 14:12). This requires that we do those things that He has called us to do.

Your life may not be going the way you want it, and then again it may be going just as you had hoped. However, God asks that you step out and do things His way. He requests that you trust Him and allow Him to direct your life (Prov. 3:5-6). You may be disappointed or angry with God because you believe that He has not intervened in your life circumstances. You may have decided to do things your way, not God's way. Remember God is the author and finisher of your success. He has begun a good work in you and will follow it through (Phil. 1:6).

Jeremiah was called to be a prophet. He was called to deliver God's Word—"Thus saith the Lord..." This was a difficult task and burdensome task for Jeremiah. On several occasions, God sent Jeremiah to deliver a word of condemnation for those who had chosen to turn from Him and not follow His way and law.

At one point in his life, Jeremiah became angry with God because he did not want to fulfill his purpose of delivering God's Word to the Israelites. He had determined that his calling was too difficult. Therefore, Jeremiah decided that he would not do as God had asked him. I believe somehow he thought it would be just that simple. You know, Lord I'm fed up, and I'm just going to do what I want to do, not what You called me to do. Oh yeah, and I hope that You will still make everything alright. This work is just too hard, depressing, and emotionally draining for me. I just can't do what You have asked of me.

God had called Jeremiah to complete this task even if he felt it was too much. Jeremiah would soon find out that he must be obedient to God's calling. God had created him for a purpose and this purpose was "caught up" in his entire existence. God had formed him in his mother's womb and had also called and

> *Like a burning fire shut up in my bones.*

sanctified him (Jer. 1:5). Jeremiah recognized that God's Word and Spirit were in his heart as a burning fire shut up in his bones (Jer. 20:9). He could not hold back from fulfilling his divine purpose. He had to deliver God's Word to His people.

God has also put your purpose in your heart—like a burning fire shut up in your bones. Be clear that God's Word and calling on your life will not return unto Him void (Isa. 55:11). You are purposed and God is "shut up in your bones!"

Faith Affirmation: *My divine purpose and destiny are like a burning fire shut up in my bones.*

Prayer: Lord, I thank You for today (Ps. 118:24). "My heart is fixed [on You]; I will sing and give praise" (Ps. 108:1) to You forever. I thank You for filling me with You, God the Holy Spirit (1 Cor. 6:19). I thank You for being like fire shut up in my bones (Jer. 20:9). I will hold on to You and go forth in Your divine purpose and plan for my life.

Dear God Letter: Talk to God about your day. Remember God's Word is like a **burning fire shut up in your bones,** guiding you to fulfill your divine purpose.

Dear God,

Date:
Day #:

STAY IN THE FIGHT

We are troubled on every side, yet not distressed; we are perplexed, but not in despair; persecuted, but not forsaken; cast down, but not destroyed (2 Cor. 4:8-9).

B ob, weave, shuffle, duck, jab, punch, bite, kick, but stay steadfast and stay in the fight. You may be experiencing a situation that feels unbearable. Maybe you have lost a loved one. Your mate has asked you for a divorce. Your child has become opposi-
tional and defiant. You are dealing with a serious illness. You lost your job. The abuse from your childhood seems to be destroying you. You can't seem to kick your bad habit or substance abuse. Your

There is a way out of the fight and that way is through Jesus Christ.

dreams and aspirations seem to be unreachable. You are experiencing feelings of guilt, shame, defeat, and you see no way out of your struggle. But, there is a way out of this fight and that way is through Jesus Christ. Jesus has already won this fight. You just have to stay in the fight. There is a blessing in it for you. You will grow stronger in your walk with God.

Jesus defeated Satan. He died on the cross and on the third day rose from the dead. He spoke to disciples saying, "All power is given unto me in heaven and in earth" (Matt. 28:18). Call out the name of Jesus, who sits on the right hand of the Father interceding for you (Rom. 8:34). Put on the whole armor of God (Eph. 6:10-18) and speak forth your faith in God. God will. God is. God has. Don't be fooled by Satan's tricks and evil doings. "Resist the devil, and he will flee from you" (Jas. 4:7). Stand firm on what you believe and trust God (Prov. 3:5-6). God is Jehovah Nisei, your victory in battle. Whatever your situation, you must remember that God has already delivered the knockout blow. You just have to stay in the fight and in God's presence. The victory is yours!

Faith Affirmation: *Lord, I will stay in the fight no matter what.*

Prayer: Lord, I thank You for another day to praise, worship and adore You (Ps. 118:24; 145:3). With You, I can face any situation because I know that I will be victorious. You reside in me and there is nothing too hard for You (1 Cor. 3:16; Gen. 18:14). You are my defense and the rock of my refuge (Ps. 94:22). "No weapon that is formed against [me] shall prosper" (Isa. 54:17).

Dear God Letter: Talk to God about your day. Remember no matter how the situation looks or feels, **stay in the fight;** you are well able to overcome in the name of Jesus.

Dear God,

Date:
Day #:

ENCOURAGE YOURSELF

And David was greatly distressed; for the people spake of stoning him,
because the soul of all the people was grieved, every man for his sons
and for his daughters: but David encouraged himself in the LORD
his God (1 Sam. 30:6).

D avid and his men returned to Ziklag, their home located in the Philistine territory (1 Sam. 27:5 – 7). It's a long story so you'll have to read it. Upon the return of the men to their home, they discovered that their town had been set on fire and their enemy, the Amalekites, had taken their wives, daughters, and sons captive. David and the men "lifted up their voice and wept, until they had no more power to weep" (1 Sam. 30:4).

David was greatly distressed because of the loss of the women and children. He was also deeply troubled because the men of his army sought to stone him. They blamed David for the capture of the women and children, "**but** David encouraged himself in the LORD his God" (1 Sam. 30:6).

I'm going to assume that David looked at his situation, and as one pastor might say, David held on to the "**but.**" He could not make heads or tails of this situation, **but** he reminded himself of God's mighty power and acts. He reminded himself to trust in the Lord.

He may have recited:
- ♥ "As the [deer] panteth after the water brooks, so panteth my soul after thee, O God" (Ps. 42:1).
- ♥ "I will love thee, O LORD my strength. The LORD is my rock, and my fortress, and my deliverer; my God, my strength, in whom I will trust; my buckler and the horn of my salvation, and my high tower" (Ps. 18:1).
- ♥ "Praise ye the LORD. Praise the LORD, O my soul. While I live will I praise the LORD . . ." (Ps. 146:1-2).

- ♥ "The LORD is my light and my salvation; whom shall I fear? The LORD is the strength of my life; of whom shall I be afraid?" (Ps. 27:1).
- ♥ "I will praise thee with my whole heart. . . Though I walk in the midst of trouble, thou will revive me: thou shall stretch forth thine hand against the wrath of mine enemies, and thy right hand shall save . . . thy mercy, O Lord, endureth forever. . ." (Ps. 138:1, 7-8).
- ♥ "I will bless the LORD at all times: His praise shall continually be in my mouth" (Ps. 34:1).
- ♥ "O taste and see that the Lord is good: blessed is the man that trusteth in Him" (Ps. 34:8).
- ♥ "The LORD is righteous in all His ways, and holy in all His works. The LORD is nigh unto all them that call upon Him, to all that call upon Him in truth. He will fulfill the desire of them that fear Him: He also will hear their cry and will save them. The Lord preserveth all them that love Him: but all the wicked will He destroy" (Ps. 145:17-20).
- ♥ "God is [my] refuge and strength, a very present help in trouble" (Ps. 46:1).
- ♥ "The LORD is on my side; I will not fear: what can man do unto me?" (Ps. 118:6).
- ♥ "My defense is of God, which [saves] the upright in heart" (Ps. 7:10).
- ♥ "Let the words of my mouth, and the meditation of my heart, be acceptable in thy sight, O LORD, my strength and my redeemer" (Ps. 19:14).

David may have also encouraged his heart with his testimony:
- ♥ It was You Oh Lord who anointed me to be king over Israel when I was just a young lad (1 Sam. 16:13).
- ♥ It was You who gave me strength to kill the bear and the lion (1 Sam. 17:34-37).
- ♥ It was You who selected the five stones from the brook and used one in my sling to kill Goliath (1 Sam. 17:40-50).
- ♥ It was You who allowed me to escape Saul's attempts to kill me (1 Sam. 19-27).
- ♥ It was You who delivered the Philistines and Amalekites into my hands and saved Your people (1 Sam. 17-30).
- ♥ It is You who have brought me thus far (Ps. 7:10). How excellent You have been in my life and will continue to be (Ps. 8:9).

♥ It is You who loves me and has wrapped Your favor around me (Ps. 5:12).

As David encouraged himself, you too can encourage yourself. Praise God for His mighty power and acts. Speak forth your testimony and encourage yourself. Remember it is "not by might, nor by power but by [God's] Spirit" (Zech. 4:6).

Faith Affirmation: *I will encourage myself in the Lord.*

Prayer: Lord, I thank You for another today to rejoice and encourage myself through my faith in You (Ps. 118:24; 1 Sam. 30:6). I will bless Your name now and for evermore (Ps. 115:18). I will rejoice in Your favor (Ps. 5:12). I will encourage myself in You. I am responsible for my reaction to the challenges of life and my response is to trust You.

Dear God Letter: Talk to God about your day. Remember **to encourage yourself in the Lord**.

Dear God,

STAY UP ON THE WALL

*And [Nehemiah] sent messengers unto [his enemies], saying, I am doing
a great work, so that I cannot come down: why should the work cease,
whilst I leave it, and come down to you? (Neh. 6:3)*

I'm up on the wall and I "canst" come down. I'm up on the wall working
to accomplish those things that God has set before me. I'm up on the
wall seeking God that I may become more like Him. While I'm on the
wall working, Satan has tried to convince me to come down so that He can
devour me. But like Nehemiah, I won't come down. I have a task to complete. I will hold God's Word in my heart and use it to stand against deception, fear, discouragement, self-doubt, despair, lust, and greed.

I'm up on the wall, and I'm walking in God's will. I'm accomplishing
God's will. God is using me to bless His people. Their lives are changing
and they're climbing up on the wall with me in the name of Jesus. I must
labor in the work of the Lord and stand guard against my enemies (Neh.
4:21-22). The Lord is my strength, and He will defeat my enemies (Ps.
27:1-5).

Stay up on the wall and don't come down. Just as Nehemiah's enemies
were trying to convince him to come down so that they could kill him.
Satan is trying to convince you to take your eyes off of Jesus so that he can
destroy you. Keep your eyes on Jesus and stay up on the wall. Satan has
been defeated, and you have the victory through Jesus Christ (Jn. 10:10).

Stay up on the wall with God's joy, faith, hope, righteousness, power,
and love. Stay up on the wall with the One who loves you. No matter the
situation, stay up on the wall with God in the name of Jesus.

Faith Affirmation: *I am up on the wall with Jesus and I "canst" come down.*

Prayer: Lord, I thank You for this day (Ps. 118:24). "Thou art my rock
and my fortress; therefore for Thy name's sake lead me and guide me" (Ps.

31:3). I am doing a great work for You and I must accomplish this work (Neh. 6:3). Your Word says, "Being confident of this very thing, that He which hath begun a good work in [me] will perform it until the day of Jesus Christ" (Phil. 1:6).

Dear God Letter: Talk to God about your day. Remember to **stay up on the wall** and don't cease the great work you are doing for God.

Dear God,

IS THERE NOT A CAUSE?

♡♡

And David said [to his brother], What have I now done? Is there not a cause? (1 Sam. 17:29)

There are so many issues that people stand up for. Sojourner Truth, a freed slave and abolitionist, stood up for the rights of African American women and men. At the 1851 Women's Rights Convention, she stood before a crowd of white women and men and proclaimed, "Ain't I a woman." She wanted the crowd to recognize that she was a woman and deserved to receive equal rights. Caesar Chavez, a prominent Mexican American labor leader and civil rights activist, fought against the injustices against migrant workers. His leadership led to migrant farm workers in California demanding and receiving better pay, and safer and improved working conditions.

Mother Teresa, a Roman Catholic nun and humanitarian, saw impoverishment in the communities she served and heard the peoples' cries for help. She established missionaries and services that provided aide to those who seemed forgotten. Mahatma Gandhi, a revered spiritual, civil rights, and humanitarian Indian leader, led the people of India as they resisted British tyranny through nonviolent civil disobedience. This nonviolent resistance led to the independence of India.

Moses stood before Pharaoh and said, "Thus saith the Lord God of Israel, Let my people go" (Ex. 5:1). Mordecai reminded Queen Esther that she had been called by God for "such a time as this" (Est. 4:14). David stood up to his brother who was insulted by his declaration that he would kill Goliath, and said, "Is there not a cause?" (1 Sam. 17:29).

Jesus was sent by God the Father to save the world (Jn. 3:16). He was crucified for no sin of His own, but for the sins of the world (1 Pet. 2:21-25). He rose from the dead with all power in His hands (Matt. 28:18) and sits at the right hand of the Father, interceding on our behalf (Rom. 8:34). God's sacrifice of His son was an act of unconditional love. There was a cause. If it had not been for this sacrifice, we would not have the gift of eternal life (Eph. 2:8-9), nor have the opportunity to live with the Father to behold His beauty and majesty.

We have been charged to spread the Good News of Jesus Christ (Matt. 28:19) and to do the work of the Lord. Have you made time to spread the love of God? Have you made time to spread the Good News of Jesus Christ? What is your response to Satan's constant attacks against you, your family, and friends? What is your response when Satan tells you to mind your own business, or this is just the way it is? What is your response to family, friends, and strangers who have not accepted Christ? What is your response to the ills of this world such as poverty, sickness, oppression, and violence? What is your response to sin? I pray your response is that there is a cause and you will lead that cause in the name of the Lord.

Is there not a cause?

Faith Affirmation: *I will stand for God's cause in the name of Jesus.*

Prayer: Lord, I thank You for another day to rejoice in Your presence (Ps. 118:24). "[You are] my strength and song, and is become my salvation" (Ps. 118:14). There is a cause and You have prepared me to fight in the name of Jesus Christ. "In [You] I have put my trust; I will not fear what [people] can do unto me" (Ps. 56:4). I will keep my heart focused on You.

Dear God Letter: Talk to God about your day. Remember, **there is a cause** and you have been called to stand and to fulfill your divine purpose in the name of Jesus.

Dear God,

CALL ON JESUS, YOUR LIFE LINE

For He shall give His angels charge over thee, to keep thee in all thy ways (Ps. 91:11).

C all on Jesus. He is always right there. Call out the name of Jesus whether you feel like it or not. His name has power. "How excellent is [His] name in all the earth!" (Ps. 8:1). The power of His name casts out demons and causes Satan to tremble. His name is above all names. The Word says, "That at the name of Jesus every knee should bow, of things in heaven, and things in earth, and things under earth; and that every tongue should confess that Jesus Christ is Lord, to the glory of God the Father" (Phil. 2:9-11). God's Word has withstood the test of time. His word is "quick, and powerful, and sharper than any two edged sword. . ." (Heb. 4:12). It cuts through spiritual warfare and through any situation. You may not feel like it's cutting through, but remember it's not a feeling; it's a fact.

God's Word is the truth. His Word is your lifeline. Just speak His name. Just call on Him, Jesus, Jesus, Jesus. Tell him how wonderful He is. How awesome He is. How much you adore Him. Tell Him all about your problems and cast them upon Him for He cares for you (1 Pet. 5:7).

Just call on Jesus.

I know you have probably heard this before, but you're hearing it again. God wants you to call on Him. He knows that the more you call Him, the more you will feel His presence. Call on Him. Call out His name. Speak the Word of God. His Word, "shall not return unto [Him] void, but it shall accomplish that which [He] please[s], and it shall prosper in the thing whereto [He] sent it" (Isa. 55:11). His Word will go forward and bless your life and the lives of others. God's Word is your lifeline; the lifeline

131

that leads to God's peace, forgiveness, love, mercy, grace, healing, righteousness, and power. Call on His name no matter what the situation or circumstance. He is "able to do exceeding abundantly above all that you ask or think according to the power that [works] within you" (Eph. 3:20).

Call God in the morning. Call Him in the noonday. Call Him in the evening. Call Him at anytime. Just call – He is waiting. Every time you call on God, you acknowledge to Him that He is King of kings and Lord of lords, the Author and Finisher of your success, the Good Shepherd, your Father and so much more.

Faith Affirmation: *I will call on the Lord, my lifeline.*

Prayer: Lord, I thank You for this day (Ps. 118:24). "I will bless [You] at all times: [Your] praise shall continually be in my mouth" (Ps. 34:1). I will "bless [thee] LORD, O my soul: and all that is within me, bless [Your] holy name" (Ps. 103:1). Without You, I can do nothing, but with You I can do all things in the name of Jesus (Phil. 4:13). I thank You that I can call on You at any time and You will answer (Isa. 65:24).

Dear God Letter: Talk to God about your day. Remember to **call on Jesus, your life line**.

Dear God,

Date:
Day #:

GOD'S ACTS OF GOODNESS

Every good gift and every perfect gift is from above, and cometh down from the Father of lights, with whom is no variableness, neither shadow of turning (Jas. 1:17).

Every good thing comes from God. These good things should remind us that God lives with us. He loves us and wants us to know that He is the God of goodness, mercy, and grace. God loves us more than we can even comprehend. His Word says that He daily loads us with His benefits (Ps. 68:19), and He shields us with his goodness and favor (Ps. 5:12). How awesome is that!

When someone tells you that you look nice, know that the comment is coming from God. When someone gives you a compliment after a meeting, know that God is complimenting you. When someone shows you an act of kindness, know that it is from God. If you do or say something good and kind, know that God has allowed you to say it to edify and build up that person. If you feel good, know that it is God's joy (Neh. 8:10). When you experience peace, thank God for releasing His peace that surpasses all understanding (Phil. 4:7). When you feel love and give love, thank God for His unconditional love. Even when you are dealing with life's challenges, remember that "all things work together for good to them that love God, to them who are the called according to his purpose" (Rom. 8:28). Acknowledge God in all things, and you will experience His goodness and love even more!

Faith Affirmation: *God shields me with His goodness and favor.*

Prayer: Lord, I thank You for this day and Your many blessings (Ps. 118:24). I will praise and worship You (Ps. 9:1). I thank You for loving me (Jn. 3:16). I thank You for all of Your acts of goodness and kindness. I

133

thank You for continuing to show me favor (Ps. 5:12). I believe that I am blessed and highly favored. I love You, Lord.

Dear God Letter: Talk to God about your day. Remember **God's acts of goodness** are full of His benefits and favor.

Dear God,

YES LORD, YES!

Serve the Lord with gladness: come before His presence with singing (Ps. 100:2).

I t is time to commit to saying yes to the Lord. Our commitment confirms that we trust and honor Him. We trust Him to direct our path and lead us to our divine purpose. We honor Him with our obedience and heartfelt thanksgiving and praise. I encourage you to make your **"Yes Lord, Yes"** commitment to the Lord today.

Yes Lord, Yes, I do love You and want to do Your will. Yes, Lord, I will do what You ask of me. It is my desire that my actions produce a sweet aroma that is pleasing to You. **Yes Lord, Yes**, I know to whom much is given much is required. I desire to do Your will and to go higher in You. **Yes Lord, Yes**, I surrender my life to You (Ps. 139:23-24). I ask You to "search me, O God, and know my heart: try me, and know my thoughts: and see if there be any wicked way in me, and lead me in the way of everlasting" (Ps. 139:23-24). **Yes Lord, Yes**, I will trust You with all my heart (Prov. 3:5-6). I will allow Your will to be done in my life (Matt. 6:9-10). I will seek You and move in my calling with an attitude of joy, a spirit of compassion, and a heart of triumph (Jn. 15:10-11; 1 Cor. 13; Jn. 16:33). **Yes Lord, Yes,** I will share the Good News of Jesus Christ (Mk. 16:15). I will bless Your name and declare that You are Wonderful, the Counselor, the mighty God, the everlasting Father, the Prince of Peace, my Lord and my Savior (Isa. 9:6). I will serve You with gladness and come before You singing songs of thanksgiving, praise, and victory for evermore (Ps. 100:2; Ps. 98:1).

Yes Lord, Yes. I know that You love me, and Your love is sweet, strong, comforting, and everlasting. It is more than sufficient, and it never fails. On this day, my soul says **Yes Lord, Yes** to Your will and to Your way.

Faith Affirmation: *Yes Lord, Yes. I say yes to Your will and yes to Your way.*

135

Prayer: Lord, I thank You for today (Ps. 118:24). I bow before You and give You the praise due unto [Your] holy name (Ps. 29:2). You are an awesome God. I say yes, Lord. Yes to Your will and yes to Your way. **Yes Lord, Yes**, I love You and want to be pleasing in Your sight (Prov. 16:7).

Dear God Letter: Talk to God about your day. Remember to answer the Father with **Yes Lord, Yes** and to let His will be done in your life.

Dear God,

Date:
Day #:

IN HIS OWN IMAGE AND LIKENESS

And God said, Let us make [humankind] in our image, after our likeness. . .
(Gen. 1:26).

God has created us in His own image and likeness (Gen. 1:26-27). The spiritual core of humankind resembles God. We are the sons and daughters of the Most High God. We must always remember that fact. We are "fearfully and wonderfully made" (Ps. 139:14). Yet at times, we question are we good enough. These thoughts of "being good enough" may come from childhood wounds. They may come from being in an abusive relationship. They also may come from a need to be liked or accepted. Whatever the origin, they still have the same negative impact. These negative thoughts hammer at your self-esteem and self-worth. They often lead you to question your abilities and God-given purpose. This questioning leads you to live below your abilities and calling. Living a mediocre or less than mediocre life becomes your way of life. Remember it's your way of life, not God's way.

You must take the time to challenge "good enough" thoughts. You know the ones: You'll never get that right. I'll stay late to make this project perfect. If it's not perfect, it's not good enough. I'll stay in this abusive relationship; it's my fault and what I deserve. I shouldn't be in this position. I'm not qualified to be a friend, wife or parent; there are others more qualified than me.

Those negative thoughts are Satan's trick to keep you from knowing how mighty and great you truly are. And, those negative thoughts are all lies. No, you are not great at everything, but you are great through Jesus Christ and the things He has called you to complete. God only sees you as His wonderful child; a child that He loves unconditionally. He loves you so much that He sent His Son to die on the cross that you would be reconciled to Him. He loves you so much that upon the crucifixion of Jesus Christ, His only begotten Son (Jn. 3:16), He left you God, the Holy Spirit. It is God, the Holy Spirit, who dwells in those who believe (1 Cor. 6:19). He comforts you, speaks to your heart, and leads you to the spiritual manifestation of His image and likeness.

God has created us in His own likeness and image.

Trust in God's view of who you are and begin to see yourself through His eyes. You are righteous. You are holy. You are created for greatness. You are "more than a conqueror through Him that love[s] us" —Christ Jesus (Rom. 8:37). Take time each day to tell yourself that you are created in God's image and likeness. You are fearfully and wonderfully made by God (Ps. 139:14). You are the perfect one for the task that God has set before you. "He who has begun a good work in you will perform unto the day of Jesus Christ" (Phil. 1:6).

Faith Affirmation: *I am fearfully and wonderfully made by God.*

Prayer: Lord, I thank You for this day (Ps. 118:24), another day to praise Your holy name (Ps. 29:2). You are my wonderful Father. I am Your child, and I thank You for loving me unconditionally. Today I walked with my head held high. I recognize that I am Your child, and "I am fearfully and wonderfully made" (Ps. 139:14). As hard as the task may seem, I acknowledge that through You I am the perfect one to complete it (Phil. 1:6).

Dear God Letter: Talk to God about your day. Remember you are a child of God, and He has **created you in His image and likeness.**

Dear God,

Date:
Day #:

DON'T LET THE
STONES CRY OUT

*And [Jesus] answered and said unto them, I tell you that, if these should
hold their peace, the stones would immediately cry out (Lk. 19:40).*

J esus is worthy to be praised. The Word says "Let everything that hath
breath praise the Lord. Praise ye the Lord" (Ps. 150:6). He is I AM
THAT I AM (Ex. 3:14). He is the bread of life (Jn. 6:48) and anyone that
believes on Him shall have everlasting life (Jn. 6:51). He is the Word. "In
the beginning was the Word, and the Word was with God, and the Word
was God. The same was in the beginning with God" (Jn. 1:1-2).

The disciples recognized and acknowledged that Jesus was the son of
the living God. They walked with Jesus and were constantly exposed to
His deity, love, might, and power. On one occasion they were traveling
with Jesus and preparing to enter Jerusalem. Many of the people in the area
heard that Jesus, the Messiah, was coming to Jerusalem. The people knew
of his miracles and awesome powers. The King of kings was coming to
Jerusalem.

The people thronged the streets anticipating the Messiah's visit. Jesus
entered Jerusalem riding on a colt, as those who were of royalty often
entered the cities. The people were hollering out His name. I can imagine
that they were crying and screaming. His
presence was overwhelming. The Word says,
"the whole multitude of the disciples began
to rejoice and praise God with a loud voice
for all the mighty works that they had seen;
saying, Blessed be the King that cometh in
the name of the Lord: peace in heaven, and
glory in the highest" (Lk. 19:37-38). Can't you see the people? Can't you
see the disciples? Can't you see Jesus riding into the town full of glory
and power?

*Jesus is worthy to be
praised.*

141

Jesus is worthy to be praised and was being praised by the disciples and the people. However, some of the Pharisees grew uncomfortable with Jesus receiving this high praise and being proclaimed king. They called out to Jesus, "Master, rebuke thy disciples" (Lk. 19:39). Basically, tell the disciples and the people to stop praising You. It's making us uncomfortable. Jesus answered them, "if these [people] shall hold their peace, [not acknowledge that I am King of kings and Lord of lords, Alpha and Omega, the Light of the Word, the Son of the Living God, the One who is to come, the Resurrection] the stones would immediately cry out" (Lk. 19:40). The stones would give me praise. For in this moment, at this point in time, I will be praised. I am the only begotten Son of God, the Messiah.

Have you praised the Lord today? Have you praised Him for His mighty acts? He is the Holy One. He sits at the right hand of the Father interceding for you (Rom. 8:34). Don't hold your praise and leave the stones to cry out. Praise Him with a loud voice for all His mighty works (Lk. 19:37). Praise Him for there is none like Him (Isa. 45:5). He has done more for you than you can imagine or comprehend. Give glory to God in the highest. Give Him his glory in every situation (Ps. 29:2). He is in every situation moving through with deity, confidence, righteousness, forgiveness, love, mercy, and grace. Take a look with your spiritual heart and eyes and you will see God. Praise Him!

Faith Affirmation: *Lord, I will praise You.*

Prayer: Lord, I thank You for this day (Ps. 118:24). You are the Most High God from everlasting to everlasting (Ps. 93:2). "Blessed be the King that cometh in the name of the Lord: peace in heaven, and glory in the highest" (Lk. 19:38). I will make a joyful noise unto the Lord – my rock and salvation (2 Sam. 22:2-3). My heart will continue to cry out "holy, holy, holy, is the LORD" (Isa. 6:3). God reigns for evermore!

Dear God Letter: Talk to God about your day. Remember to stop and praise God. **Don't let anything or anybody cry out** praises to the Lord, because you refuse to give Him the praise that is due His name.

Dear God,

Date:

Day #:

THE BEST MADE DECISION AND PLAN

There is a way which seemeth right unto a man; but the end thereof are the ways of death (Prov. 14:12).

For the past months, I have been reflecting on a decision that I made. When I made the decision, I believed it to be the right decision and subsequently I didn't leave room for anyone to guide me differently. **Now that I'm living with the consequences of my decision, I believe I must have lost my mind.** What was I thinking? Why hadn't I considered the "what ifs" of my plan? My best made decision had plenty of holes, I just couldn't see them. I had deceived myself. I really think that I had lost my mind. The situation was a bit much and I allowed my fear to guide my final decision.

I have been seeking God about this matter and praying for peace and fortitude. I had sought Him before I made my final decision, but I made the final decision and just hoped He would bless it. I have had to encourage myself, forgive myself, and trust God to take my mess and make it into something good. His Word says, "And we know that all things work together for good to them that love God, to them who are the called according to His purpose" (Rom. 8:28). The Lord reminded me that there is nothing new under the sun (Eccles. 1:9). He reminded me that I'm not the first to develop a "best made plan."

God took me to Abraham who told the Egyptian Pharaoh that Sarah, his wife and half-sister, was his sister rather than his wife. Sarah was beautiful and Abraham feared the Egyptians would kill him so that they could take Sarah as their handmaiden or wife (Gen. 12:11-13), but they would not need to kill him if he presented Sarah as his sister. The Egyptians did acknowledge Sarah's beauty just as Abraham had predicted. Sarah was taken to Pharaoh's house so that he could take her as his wife. In response to Pharaoh's request to have Sarah become his wife, the Lord plagued

145

Pharaoh and his house with great plagues because this was not His plan for Abraham and Sarah (Gen. 12:16-17). He had chosen Abraham to be the father of many nations (Gen. 17: 1-4). Pharaoh called Abraham and questioned him saying, "What is this that you have done unto me? Why didst thou not tell me that [Sarah] was your wife?" (Gen. 12:18). In today's language, Pharaoh was asking, "What type of sick trick are you playing?" Then Pharaoh ordered Abraham to take Sarah and leave.

In the plains of Mamre, three angels visited Abraham. They told him that Sarah would have a son (Gen. 18:10). Now, Sarah heard the angels tell Abraham of the promise of a son (Gen. 18:10-11) and because she was old and beyond childbearing years, she laughed within herself (Gen. 18:12). "And the Lord said unto Abraham, Wherefore did Sarah laugh. . . Is anything too hard for the Lord?" (Gen. 18:12-14).

As time passed, Sarah became impatient waiting to conceive the son that the Lord had promised to her and Abraham. Sarah encouraged her husband to sleep with his handmaiden, Hagar, and Hagar bore a son Ishmael. Now, this was not God's plan but a "best made decision and plan" developed out of the impatience and fear of Abraham and Sarah. The decision to birth a child outside of God's covenant with Abraham would lead to Ishmael not receiving the rights of the firstborn son, being cast from the tribe of Abraham, and God establishing another nation because Ishmael was Abraham's seed (Gen. 21).

In time, Sarah became pregnant and her son was called Isaac, which fulfilled the promise and plan that God made to Abraham. Sarah would conceive a son, Isaac, and Abraham's seed would be as innumerable as the stars (Gen. 15:1-6). Isaac received the firstborn status and became the forefather of

We must seek God and allow Him to reveal His plan.

the Jews. Out of Abraham's and Sarah's impatience and fear, they developed and implemented a "best made plan" that created strife and loss. Yet, God intervened and upheld the covenant that He made with Abraham. What a mighty and sovereign God.

There is no best made plan made by humankind. We must seek God and allow Him to reveal His plan. If God called it, He is faithful and just to fulfill it (1 Thess. 5:24). God's Word "shall not return unto Him void, but it shall accomplish that which He please[s]" (Isa. 55:11). Take the time to talk with God about His plan for your life. Take the time to just sit with God. Give Him an opportunity to talk with you. God will answer your prayers.

If you already know that you are the one who created and implemented your plan (1) Ask God for forgiveness; (2) Forgive yourself; (3) Seek God diligently (4) Trust God, and (5) Allow God to reveal His plan and order your footsteps (Ps. 37:23; Ps. 119:133-135). His way is the only way (Ps. 18:32). His way is the best made plan for your life and the world.

Faith Affirmation: *I will wait on the Lord and only follow the plan He has for my life.*

Prayer: Lord, I rejoice knowing that this is the day that You created for me (Ps. 118:24). It was a day full of many benefits seen and unseen (Ps. 68:19). Lord, it is Your plan that I walk with You and come to my expected end (Jer. 29:11). It is my desire to do Your will. Help me, O Lord to be patient and wait on You.

Dear God Letter: Talk to God about your day. Remember, because God loves you, He has established **a best made decision and plan** that can only work out for your good.

Dear God,

Date:
Day #:

CALL ON ME

He shall call upon me, and I will answer him: I will be with him in trouble; I will deliver him, and honor him (Ps. 91:15).

O n Monday, I ran into a problem that really bothered me, but I did not do anything about it. On Tuesday, I woke up with the spirit of anxiety that was connected to my Monday problem, but I did not do anything about it. On Wednesday, I danced with the spirit of fear. On Thursday, I slept with both the spirit of anxiety and fear, but I did not do anything about it. I guess I thought they would just go away. On Friday, I woke up and I felt the spirit of depression and had a hard time getting my day started. On Saturday, the spirits of helplessness, hopelessness, and despair joined their partners, anxiety, fear, and depression. I felt like I had just run into a brick wall that had come out of nowhere.

On Sunday, I woke up and thought what's happening to me. Lord, please help me. That morning, I dragged myself out of bed and went to church. On my way to church, the spirits of anxiety, fear, and despair tried to convince me to turn around and go back home. The Holy Spirit continued to direct me to church. When I arrived at the church, I immediately felt the peace of God. He reminded me that I was His child and He loved me. He had not given me the spirit of fear but of power, love and a sound mind (2 Tim. 1:7). I did not need to have a troubled heart. He was with me (1 Cor. 6:19) and would remain with me always and forever (Matt. 28:20).

I dropped my head and began to weep. God offered me His perfect peace, love, and grace. In that moment, I was no longer entangled in the yoke of bondage (Gal. 5:1). I could feel God's love deep inside of me. I knew that I was safe with my Father. With a heart of gratitude and love, I sang a love song unto the Lord, and I praised and worshiped Him. Then, I just sat quietly with the Lord and my tears flowed as His presence embraced me. The Lord's final words to me that morning were "I am always near and will always love you. Remember to call on me. I will answer and deliver you" (Ps. 91:15).

Because we face adversities and trials in life, we will have days that we don't know exactly what happened or why we're feeling a certain way. In those times, pause and call on the Lord, in the name of Jesus. His Word says that He is with you in times of trouble. If you call on Him, He will answer. He will deliver you, and He will honor you (Ps. 91:15). No matter the situation you are victorious through Christ Jesus. Call on Jesus. He is just a breath away.

Faith Affirmation: *I will call on Jesus, my Lord and Savior.*

Prayer: Lord, I thank You for another day to call out to You and to rejoice knowing that You will answer (Ps. 118:24; Ps. 91:15). I will "bless [You] Lord, O my soul: and all that is within me, [I will] bless [Your] holy name" (Ps. 103:1). I will call on You for there is no other help I know. I will call on You no matter the situation, and You will deliver me (Ps. 91:15). With long life, You will satisfy me and show me Your salvation (Ps. 91:16).

Dear God Letter: Talk to God about your day. **Call on the Lord**. He will answer and deliver you.

Dear God,

PRAISE AND WORSHIP ALL DAY LONG

O Praise the LORD. . .for His merciful kindness is great toward us. . .
O come, let us worship and bow down: let us kneel before the LORD
our maker (Ps. 117:1-2; 95:6).

D avid was committed to praising and worshipping the Lord. He
desired to have an intimate relationship with Him. David made a
commitment to praise and worship the Lord all day long. His praise came
from His love and appreciation of God. David had experienced the presence, favor, and power of the Lord. He knew who he was and who he would
become was ordained by God. He also knew what God had done for him,
and what God would do for him. He honored His Creator and sought to
please Him.

David's praise to the Lord gave him great strength, peace, and comfort.
His praise sustained him and lifted his soul, as he awaited God's deliverance. His praise also showed his dependence on his Father and acknowledged that God was the keeper of his life (Ps. 121:5), and the One who
would "preserve [his] going out and [his] coming in from this time forth,
and even for evermore" (Ps. 121:8).

Your love for the Father will also produce a heart of praise and worship.
Let praise be who you are and what you do. The more you praise Him, the
more opportunities you have to worship Him and enter into His presence.
"God is a Spirit: and they that worship Him must worship Him in spirit and
in truth" (Jn. 4:24). With a spirit of love and liberty, you can praise and
worship God and allow His anointing to rest and abide with you. Through
your praise God will be glorified; your spirit will be uplifted, and you will
enjoy the love and presence of your Father.

Your praise will bring you through any situation and into a spirit of
worship and victory. Come with expectancy; come with a heart of praise

and worship. For some will thank God for what He has done and some will worship God because of who He is. You were created to give God glory (Isa. 43:7), and He inhabits (occupies) your praises (Ps. 22:3). When you truly praise and worship God, you surrender to Him. From the depths of your heart and soul, confess that He is GOD Almighty. He is the Lord of your life. He is God alone, and there is none like Him (Ps. 86:10; Isa. 45:5). Oh, come and praise, worship and adore Him all day long. He is Christ our Lord!

Faith Affirmation: *I will praise and worship the Lord.*

Prayer: Lord, I thank You for this day; another day to praise You (Ps. 118:24; 150:6). Lord, I will give You "the glory due unto [Your] name; [and] worship [You] in the beauty of holiness" (Ps. 29:2) from this day forward. "How excellent is [Your] name in all the earth!" (Ps. 8:1). You are righteous and holy (1 Pet. 1:16). You are great and greatly to be praised (Ps. 145:3). I thank You for giving me a heart of praise, thanksgiving, and worship. All the days of my life, I will praise and worship You, my Lord and Savior.

Dear God Letter: Talk to God about your day. Remember **to praise and worship the Lord all day long**. He is worthy to be praised.

Dear God,

LET IT GO

Now the Lord is that Spirit: and where the Spirit of the Lord is, there is liberty (2 Cor. 3:17).

L et It Go
LET It Go
LET IT GO!
Have you Let It Go Yet?
You know the matter that's causing your stomach to turn and your head to ache.
The concern that's invading your thoughts and keeping you awake all night.
The thing that's keeping your blood pressure high and you on edge.
That thing that's smothering your peace and joy;
That thing that's causing you to take your eye off of God;
That thing that's causing you to question the love and presence of your Father;
That thing that's causing you to quench the Holy Spirit;
That thing that just won't stop.

Let It Go
Let It Go
Satan comes "but for to steal, and to kill, and to destroy" (Jn. 10:10).
God came that "[you] might have life, and that [you] might have it more abundantly" (Jn. 10:10).
God is near and at hand (Phil. 4:5).
He requests that you "[cast] all your care upon Him; for He careth for [you]" (1 Pet. 5:7).
It is God's will that you surrender your situation to Him and "count it all joy" knowing that God will work it out (Jas. 1:2-4).
Trust in God and "be [anxious] for nothing!" (Phil. 4:6).

Let It Go
Release It
Release It to God
Grab hold of His joy, love, peace, hope, mercy, and grace.
Speak forth your faith and surrender your situation to God
(Matt. 11: 28-30).
Meditate on those thoughts that are true, honest, and lovely (Phil. 4:8).
Create positive images that lift your spirit and comfort your soul.
Embrace God who loves you! (Jer. 31:3)

Let It Go
Release It
Give It to God and reach to Jesus Christ (Col. 3:1-2), the rock of your
salvation (2 Sam. 22:2-3) and author and finisher of your faith (Heb. 12:2)
and life.
He will do "exceeding abundantly above all that [you] ask or think,
according to the power that worketh in [you]" (Eph. 3:20).
He will because He is God!

Faith Affirmation: *I am letting go of my situation and holding on to Jesus.*

Prayer: Lord, I thank You for another day to rejoice and be glad (Ps.
118:24). You are my strength and my redeemer (Ps. 19:14). You are always
with me (Matt. 28:20). I will let my life situations go and count them all joy
knowing that You will make a way for me (Jas. 1:2-4). You dwell within
me (1 Cor. 3:16), "and where the Spirit of the Lord is, there is liberty" (2
Cor. 3:17).

Dear God Letter: Talk to God about your day. The Spirit of the Lord gives
you the power to **let it go**.

Dear God,

PRESSING

The thief cometh not, but for to steal, and to kill, and to destroy:
I am come that they might have life, and that they might have it
more abundantly (Jn. 10:10).

I was watching the movie Tombstone, which is a western movie based on the legend of U.S. Marshall Wyatt Earp and Doc Holiday. If you like Westerns, this is one you may want to check out. Wyatt Earp and Doc Holiday lived quite intense lives. Their lives included marriage, divorce, law enforcement, gunfights, drinking, sex, gambling, disappointment, illness, love, death, and so much more.

At the end of the movie, Wyatt Earp visits Doc Holiday, who is dying in the hospital. During this visit with Doc Holiday, Wyatt Earp shared his concerns about his next steps in life. He tells Doc that he wished he had lived a normal life. Doc replies, "There is no such thing as a normal life, there is just life." This is so true. There is no such thing as a normal life. Life is full of ups and downs, happy times and not so happy times, living and dying, exuberance and sadness, sickness and health, prosperity and poverty, disappointments and victories, light and darkness; need I go on? Life is just that –It's life.

When life is going great, we often think we are living a normal life. We are happy and content. We have an attitude of expectancy and victory. We praise and rejoice in the Lord. However, when times get tough, you know— job loss, loss of a loved one, financial problems, relationship issues, dream disappointments— we think we're not living a normal life. We begin to question ourselves and wonder how we will ever make it through. We stop anticipating God's favor and victory. However, what we need to do is encourage ourselves and **press in the name of Jesus**.

Press in the morning, afternoon and evening. Press through the disappointment to happiness. Press through the hurt and pain to joy and laughter. Press through the thoughts of defeat to victory. Press to have life and have it more abundantly. **Press, Press, Press**. Make yourself get up each day with an attitude and heart to press. Yell it out loud; I am pressing in the name of the Jesus. I am pressing because there is nothing too hard or impossible for God (Matt. 19:26). I am pressing to overcome feelings of defeat. I am God's child, and He knows my position in life and will change it only for my good. My best days are yet to come.

> *I am pressing in the name of Jesus.*

Keep your thoughts on those things that are good, right, just and pure (Phil. 4:8). Keep your thoughts on the goodness of God and all that He has done and will do. It's not easy, but **Press, Press, Press**. Did I say **Press**? **God has been good to you, and He will accomplish His good work in you** (Phil. 1:6). Press to obtain more of an abundance of hope, strength, and courage. Press, in the name of the Lord, again, I say to you, **Press, Press, Press** to a new level of trust and faith in God. What would it hurt? NOTHING! It can only benefit you; for God came "that [you] might have life, and that [you] might have it more abundantly" (Jn. 10:10). **PRESS!**

Faith Affirmation: *I am pressing to my victory in the name of Jesus.*

Prayer: Lord, I thank You for this day (Ps. 118:24), another day to press and to do Your will. "How excellent is [Your] name in all the earth!"(Ps. 8:1). I press in the name of Jesus to receive my more than abundant life. "I press toward the mark for the prize of the high calling of God in Christ Jesus" (Phil. 3:14). I press to receive my victory in Jesus Christ.

Dear God Letter: Talk to God about your day. **Keep pressing** in the Spirit. The power of the Holy Spirit works in you as you press in the name of Jesus.

Dear God,

Date:
Day #:

AN ISSUE OF BLOOD

And a woman having an issue of blood twelve years, which had spent all
her living upon physicians, neither could be healed of any, came behind
him, and touched the border of his garment: and immediately her issue
of blood [stopped] (Lk. 8:43-48).

D o you have an issue that you're struggling with? You know an issue
that you have tried to overcome. This issue could be something
such as an addiction, troubling thoughts, worry, a negative attitude, disappointment, an illness, or a broken heart. You have talked to your family
and friends about your issue. You have read self-help books. You have
read Christian books. You have talked to your physician or counselor about
your issue. You gone to treatment, inpatient and outpatient. You have
even talked to strangers about your issue, but to no avail; your issue seems
to have a life and mind of its own. In fact, one time you were headed to
recovery, only for your issue to reappear more pronounced.

There was a woman in the Bible who had an issue, an issue of blood.
For twelve years she had been afflicted by some type of illness that caused
continuous bleeding. She had gone to physicians, but they could not find a
cure. I would assume they gave her instructions on what she should do if
she wanted to stop the bleeding. They probably prescribed different types
of herbs and medicines. She may have also received advice from women
in the community. Yet, the woman continued to bleed.

You can imagine that the woman who had this issue of blood, had to
spend a lot of time taking care of this illness. She may have wondered if this
illness would be with her for the rest of her life. Would she die from this
illness? Some people may have shunned her because of her illness. At times,
she may have become depressed. This illness was seriously impacting her
quality of life. There had to be someone or something that could heal her.

Somehow and somewhere, this woman heard about Jesus, the Messiah.
I'm assuming she heard the stories of how he had healed the sick, lame,

161

blind, and raised people from the dead. He was the only begotten son of God – a miracle worker. If she could meet him, surely He would heal her. He was her only hope.

The word spread that Jesus was coming to town. This was the opportunity that she was waiting for. A multitude of people met Him at the shore. He had been in another city healing people and casting out demons. The people in the crowd cried out to Jesus and pressed him on every side (Lk. 8:40, 42). The woman with the issue of blood was among the people in the crowd who were pushing and pressing to get close to the Messiah. She so desperately wanted to be healed. It was now or never. With all of her might, she pressed through the crowd, reached toward Jesus with her hand and heart of faith, and touched the hem of His holy garment. But she had touched more than just the hem of His garment. She had touched His heart.

Jesus responded immediately, "Someone [has] touched me: for I perceive that [power] is gone out of me" (Lk. 8:46). In that moment, she realized that even though there was a multitude of people pressing against Jesus, He knew someone had touched Him, and had been healed. With trepidation, she stepped forward and acknowledged to Jesus and all the people why she had touched Him and that she had been healed (Lk. 8:47). Jesus said unto her, "Daughter, be of good [cheer]: thy faith has made you whole; go in peace" (Lk. 8:48). The woman had touched Jesus' heart. I believe that the faith and determination in her heart connected with the heart of Jesus, which connected to the heart of God. Hallelujah!

Seek God with a heart of faith.

You don't have to wait for Jesus to come through the crowd. God lives within you (1 Cor. 3:16). But, you may have to press through your own doubt, discouragement, and disappointments. Press in the name of Jesus and rebuke any obstacles that would hinder your progress. Believe that you will be healed in the name of Jesus. God desires that you would live a full, healthy and prosperous life. However, this does require that you deal with the issues of life. Your only hope to resolve them requires that you seek God with a heart of faith. Your healing and deliverance will occur beyond what you could have imagined.

Faith Affirmation: *I am reaching for God with a heart of faith.*

Prayer: Lord, I thank You for today (Ps. 118:24). I know that You have heard my prayers and will heal me. I praise Your name (Ps. 113). You are "my strength and my redeemer" (Ps. 19:14). I thank You for healing me. You are the only One who has the power to heal. It is "with [Your] stripes that [I am] healed" (Isa. 53:5).

Dear God Letter: Talk to God about your day. God is the answer to your **issue of blood**. He is your healer and deliverer.

Dear God,

Date:
Day #:

I BELIEVE

. . . two blind men followed [Jesus], crying, and saying, Thou son of David have mercy on us . . . and Jesus saith unto them, Believe ye that I am able to do this? They said unto him, Yea, Lord. Then touched He their eyes, saying According to your faith be it unto you. And their eyes were opened. . . (Matt. 9:27-30).

I Believe
I believe in You Lord
I believe Jesus Christ is the ONLY begotten son of God
(Lk. 1:29-32).
I believe that You are the only Savior (Isa. 43:11).
I believe that You love me always and for evermore (1 Jn. 4:10).
I believe that Your love never fails (Lam. 3:22).
I believe in You Lord!

As I move and breathe, I believe that:
- ♥ Only You have the power to heal the sick and mend broken hearts (Lk. 4:18).
- ♥ You are "able to do exceeding abundantly above all that [I] ask or think, according to the power that worketh in [me]" (Eph. 3:20).
- ♥ My God-given gifts and talents will bless Your people and me (1 Cor. 12:1-11).
- ♥ You love me, and You will do what You said You will do (Isa. 55:11).

As I call out Your name, I believe that:
- ♥ You hear my prayers, and You answer them (Jas. 5:13-16).
- ♥ Whatsoever I ask in Your name, it shall be done (Jn. 14:12-14).
- ♥ There is nothing too hard for You (Gen. 18:14).
- ♥ "With [You] all things are possible" (Matt. 19:26).
- ♥ You make the difference in my life (2 Cor. 5:17).

With my whole heart, I believe that:

- ♥ You called me "for such a time as this" (Est. 4:14).
- ♥ I am surrounded by Your favor like a shield (Ps. 5:12).
- ♥ You "daily loadeth [me] with benefits" (Ps. 68:19).
- ♥ You have plans for me, plans that I would prosper (Jer. 29:11).
- ♥ You love me, Oh, how You love me, and
- ♥ There is nothing that shall separate me from Your love (Rom. 8:38-39).

I believe in You!

Faith Affirmation: *I believe in You Lord.*

Prayer: Lord, I thank You for today (Ps. 118:24). I will praise Your name forever (Ps. 29:1-2). I believe that Jesus Christ is the Son of God (Rom. 10:9). I believe that there is "one God and Father of all, who is above all, and through all, and in [us] all" (Eph. 4:6). I believe in Your power and miracles. I believe that You are all that I need. I believe in You! (Matt. 16:14-16)

Dear God Letter: Talk to God about your day. **I believe that You are the son of God, my Lord and Savior.**

Dear God,

Date:
Day #:

GET UP

Let your conversation be without covetousness; and be content with such things as ye have: for He hath said, I will never leave thee nor forsake thee. So that we can boldly say, the Lord is my helper, and I will not fear what man shall do unto me (Heb. 13:5-6).

As Christians, we will face adversities that leave us feeling like we've fallen down or failed. We may feel like our worst nightmare has come upon us –our worst fear has come to pass. You know the hidden fear of death, bankruptcy, job termination, terminal illness, divorce, mental illness, or being exposed.

Just know that when you fall or fail, God is right there. He said, "I will never leave thee, nor forsake thee" (Heb. 13:5). He will never leave nor turn His heart from you. God loves you always and forever. In the midst of your fall, call on the name of Jesus Christ. His name is a "strong tower: the righteous runneth into it, and is safe" (Prov. 18:10).

For every fall, or perceived failure, God has a soothing word and has already made a way out. You may say, "Lord my mate left me." The Lord replies, "I love you and have the power to mend your heart." Lord, "I lost my job." He replies "I have not seen the righteous forsaken, nor my seed begging for bread" (Ps. 37:25). Lord, "I'm just tired." The Lord replies, "Come unto me, all ye that labor and are heavy laden, and I will give you rest" (Matt. 11:28). Lord, "I've lost my way. I don't know which way to turn." The Lord replies, "[My] word is a lamp unto [your] feet, and a light unto [your] path" (Ps. 119:105). Lord, "I am broken hearted." The Lord replies, "I love you and will comfort you. I am the God of all Comfort" (2 Cor. 1:3). Lord, "I have been diagnosed with a terminal illness." The Lord replies, "I love you. Have faith in me (Mk. 11:22). It is I who has the power over life and death (Matt. 28:18). I hold your destiny in my loving hands." Whatever your adversity, God remains King of kings and Lord of lords. Trust in the Lord!

Faith Affirmation: *The Lord is always with me.*

Prayer: Lord, I thank You for this day (Ps. 118:24). You are a wonderful Father and protector (Ps. 61:3). I thank You for loving me unconditionally (1 Jn. 4:10). I thank You for always being there to pick me up (Heb. 13:5-6). I thank You for giving me the courage to get back up again and again. "[Your] mercies] are new every morning: great is thy faithfulness" (Lam. 3:22-23). I love You, Lord.

Dear God Letter: Talk to God about your day. **Get up** and boldly declare that God is your helper.

Dear God,

Date:
Day #:

SO, SO WHAT, WHATEVER

Casting all your care upon Him; for He careth for you (1 Pet. 5:7).

A t some point in your Christian walk, you must arrive at a place of trusting and believing in the Lord to the point that you can look a stressful situation in the eye and say **So**, God has always made a way out of no way. **So, so what,** God will provide. **So, so what,** "I can do all things through Christ which strengthens me" (Phil. 4:13). I will not be moved. **So, so what, whatever,** this too shall pass. I have the victory in the name of Jesus.

You should take a moment to yell out, **so, so what, whatever**. You should begin to practice these words. Get them in your spirit and the forefront of your mind so that you are prepared to say **so what**, God has covered me with his shield of favor (Ps. 5:12), and I shall not be moved. **Whatever, whatever,** Satan is a liar and deceiver. I have faith that God will see me through. I "cast all [my] care upon Him; for He careth for me" (1 Pet. 5:7). **So, so what, whatever,** "in all things [I] am more than a conqueror through Him that loved [me]" (Rom. 8:37).

The more you say **so, so what, whatever**, the more you acknowledge that you trust in the Lord. The more you say **so, so what, whatever**, the more you surrender unto God's will. The more you say **so, so what, whatever**, the more you are strengthened to continue to climb the mountain. The more you say **so, so what, whatever**, the more you stop the murmuring and complaining and stay focused on God and His Word of victory. God will reward you for your faith and obedience (Heb. 11:6). You have the victory in the name of Jesus.

Faith Affirmation: *So, so what- whatever, God is able.*

Prayer: Lord, I thank You for this day (Ps. 118:24). You are loving, strong, and mighty (Ps. 24:8). I am Your child and I thank You for loving me unconditionally (1 Jn. 4:10). I thank You for the privilege to "cast all my care upon [You] for [You] careth for me" (1 Pet. 5:7). I know that I will have trials and tribulation, but I must trust You and believe that all things will work together for my good (Rom. 8:28). Lord, I love You.

Dear God Letter: Talk to God about your day. The more you can say and believe **"so, so, what – whatever"** the more you acknowledge that God has the answer that will work out for your good.

Dear God,

Date:
Day #:

RUN TO THE LINE OF THE ENEMY

♡♡

And it came to pass, when the Philistine arose, and came, and drew nigh
to meet David, that David hastened, and ran toward the army to meet
the Philistine (1 Sam. 17:48).

D avid knew that Goliath was trying to back him and the men of God
off the battlefield line and send them all running in fear. Goliath had
been successful with causing fear amongst the men of the armies of the
living God. Goliath came to the battlefield with the Philistine army ready
to defeat the armies of Israel. Goliath would execute any and all battle
tactics to get the job done, including "talking smack" in hopes of getting
into the minds of his opponents. Goliath knew that the battle was not only
physical but also mental.

David knew the battle was the Lord's! David kept his mind and heart
focused on what God had done and what God would do. This caused him
to have an attitude of victory! Goliath was just a big man to David and
nothing more. David knew that Goliath and the Philistines were no match
for the Lord of Hosts. Just as God had allowed him to slay the bear and the
lion, he would slay Goliath (1 Sam. 17:34-37).

God had prepared David for just this moment. David took his staff in
his hand, and chose five smooth stones out of the brook, and put them in his
shepherd's bag and his sling in his hand and drew near unto the Philistines
with confidence. He knew that God would deliver him and the armies of
Israel from this uncircumcised Philistine; therefore, he need not get overwhelmed. David hurried and ran toward the army to meet Goliath (1 Sam.
17:40, 48). "And David put his hand in his bag, and took [out] a stone, and
slang it, and [struck] the Philistine in his forehead" (1 Sam. 17:49) and the
rest is history. Goliath was killed and the Philistines were defeated.

171

God is asking you to take Him to the battlefield line. The battle is between God and Satan. If you take God to the line, He will deliver you from Satan's strongholds of fear, shame, low self-esteem, depression, despair, anger, perfectionism, addiction, abuse, loneliness, and so forth. Today and every day fill your heart (shepherd's bag) with those scriptures that God has given you for the battle. Each scripture is a weapon from God that can be used to defeat Goliath and the Philistines. Each scripture is filled with God's power, peace, and victory. Make haste toward the enemy and release God's Word. His Word "shall not return unto Him void, but it shall accomplish that which [pleases God], and it shall prosper in the thing whereto [He] sent it" (Isa. 55:11). The battle is the Lord's!

> *The enemy is no match for the Lord of Hosts.*

Faith Affirmation: *I will run to the line for the battle is the Lord's.*

Prayer: Lord I thank You for this day (Ps. 118:24), another day to praise Your holy name (Ps. 29:2). You are a wonderful Father and protector (Ps. 61:3). I thank You for loving me unconditionally (1 Jn. 4:10). I thank You for giving me all that I need to run to the line (1 Sam. 17:48). I thank You for the courage to fight in the name of Jesus. I thank You for always being with me and defeating my enemies (Ps. 18:39). I am so grateful to have You in my life.

Dear God Letter: Talk to God about your day. You can **run to the line of the enemy** knowing that the battle is the Lord's, and you will come out victorious!

Dear God,

Date:
Day #:

MORE THAN CONQUERORS

Nay, in all these things we are more than conquerors through Him that loved us (Rom. 8:37).

Those folks who love God and are called according to His purpose are **more than** conquerors. Upon David's defeat of Goliath and the subsequent defeat of the Philistines, the Israelites hailed David as a conqueror and great leader. "And Saul set David over the men of war, and he was accepted in the sight of all the people, and also in the sight of Saul's servants" (1 Sam. 18:5). When David entered the cities of Israel after his defeat of the Philistines, "the women came out of the cities of Israel, singing and dancing . . . the women answered one another as they played, and said, Saul hath slain his thousands, and David his ten thousands" (1 Sam. 18:6-7). In the eyes of the people, David was a great conqueror.

In the eyes of God, David was **more than** a conqueror; just as you are more than a conqueror. How can someone be more than a conqueror? You can only be **more than** a conqueror through Jesus Christ, our Lord and Savior. You are **more than** a conqueror because you are a child of God, and God lives within you (1 Cor. 3:16). You are **more than** a conqueror because "Greater is He that is in you than he that is in the world" (1 Jn. 4:4). You are **more than** a conqueror because death cannot hold you, the believer. As a believer, you are destined to great works and to live with the Father in heaven (Jn. 11:25-26; 14:12). Always, remember that in the eyes of God, you are **more than** a conqueror.

Faith Affirmation: *I am more than a conqueror through Christ Jesus.*

Prayer: Lord, I thank You for today (Ps. 118:24), another day to be more than a conqueror through You (Rom. 8:37). You are excellent and worthy to be praised (Ps. 8:1). I love You, Lord. You are "my rock, and my fortress, and my deliverer; my God, my strength, in whom I will trust. . ." (Ps. 18:1-2). I am Your child, and I thank You for loving me unconditionally.

Dear God Letter: Talk to God about your day. Tell Him all about it. **You are more than a conqueror** in the name of Jesus.

Dear God,

GOD'S LOVE

. . . for God is love (1 Jn. 4:8).

G od is love. Love is of God and from God. He loves you so much that He gave His only begotten son, Jesus Christ, to die for your sins and save the world (1 Jn. 4:8-10). God knew that His son's death would leave His children comfortless and without guidance. With His perfect love, He sent His Spirit, the Holy Spirit, to dwell in you (1 Cor. 3:16) and guide you into your divine calling and purpose. Now, that's love.

God, who is love, will never leave nor forsake you (Heb. 13:5). Paul wrote, "For I am persuaded, that neither death, nor life, nor angels, nor principalities, nor powers, nor things present, nor things to come, nor height, nor depth, nor any other creature, shall be able to separate us from the love of God, which is in Christ Jesus our Lord" (Rom. 8:38-39). God offers His unconditional and steadfast love to you. It is His desire that you would receive His *Nothing can separate us from God's love.* love and that you would love Him. It is His hope that you would open your heart and allow His love to draw you to Him. It is God's love that offers you His gift of eternal salvation and everlasting life (Jn. 3:16; Eph. 2:8-9).

God's love is one thing that you can hold onto forever. Take the time to experience, appreciate, and acknowledge God's amazing love. His love is filled with His power and will never fail (Lam. 3:22). God's love is filled with everything you need or could imagine. His love invites you to surrender your all and become more like Him. His love is from everlasting to everlasting. God loves you. Oh, how He loves you!

Faith Affirmation: *God loves me more than I am able to comprehend.*

Prayer: Lord, I thank You for today (Ps. 118:24), another day to praise You with all of my heart (Ps. 9:1). You are love (1 Jn. 4:8). You love me (1 Jn. 4:10). I love You (1 Jn. 4:19). Your love is amazing and everlasting (Jer. 31:3). I thank You for giving me the power to love (1 Jn. 4:12). I am grateful that there is nothing that can separate me from Your love (Rom. 8:35-39).

Dear God Letter: Talk to God about your day. **God's love** is perfect and never fails.

Dear God,

Date:
Day #:

THE NAMES OF GOD
HAVE POWER

The name of the Lord is a strong tower: the righteous runneth into it, and is safe (Prov.18:10). O LORD, our Lord how excellent is thy name in all the earth! (Ps. 8:1)

There is power in the names of God. Only God's names have the power to protect, heal, comfort and save us. Call out the names of God in your time of trouble and as you praise and worship Him. God loves you and is ever present, just call out His name and experience His love and power.

Adonai (Lord) – *pronunciation: A-doh-nay.* God is our Lord and offers us His love, goodness, and blessings. David wrote, "I sought the Lord, and He heard me, and delivered me from all my fears. . . O taste and see that the LORD is good: blessed is the [person] that trusteth in Him" (Ps. 34:4 & 8).

El Elyon (Most High God) – *pronunciation: El Elee-yon.* He is the Most High God and reigns forever (Rev. 11:15). "For thou, LORD, art high above all the earth: thou art exalted far above all gods" (Ps. 97:9). "It's a good thing to give thanks unto the LORD. . . O Most High" (Ps. 92:1-2).

El Emunah (The Faithful God) – *pronunciation: El Eh-moo-nah.* He is the faithful God. He will do what He said He would do. "Know therefore that the LORD thy God, He is God, the faithful God, which keepeth covenant and mercy with them that love Him and keep His commandments to a thousand generations" (Deut. 7:9).

El Gibor (Mighty God) – *pronunciation: El Kee-bor.* God is a Mighty (powerful, strong) God. "The name of the LORD is a strong tower: the righteous [run] into it, and is safe" (Prov. 18:10).

179

El Kanna (Jealous God) – *pronunciation: El Kan-nah*. God is our Creator, and He is a jealous God. "For thou shalt worship no other god: for the LORD, whose name is Jealous, is a jealous God" (Ex. 34:14).

El Olam (The Everlasting God) – *pronunciation: El O-lam*. There is no beginning or end to God; He is everlasting to everlasting. David wrote, "The LORD reigneth, He is clothed with majesty (Ps. 93:1) . . . thy throne is established of old: thou art from everlasting" (Ps. 93:2).

El Roi (The God Who Sees) – *pronunciation: El Raw-ee*. God is omnipresent and sees everything. Hagar, Sarai's slave, who finds herself lost, pregnant, and desperate cries out to the Lord. In her weakest and darkest moment, she recognizes that God sees all, and He has not lost sight of her (Gen. 16:3). God sees us and knows our heart. He watches over His children. If His eye is on the sparrow, surely He watches over you (Matt. 10:29-31).

El Shaddai (The Almighty God; The All Sufficient God) – *pronunciation: El Shaddai*. God is almighty and more than enough. God has sovereignty over this world and our lives. God established Himself as the Almighty God to Abram, with whom He later established an everlasting covenant and renamed him Abraham, the father of many nations (Gen. 17:1-5). "Now unto [God] that is able to do exceeding abundantly above all that we ask or think, according to the power that worketh in us" (Eph. 3:20).

Elohim (The Creator) – *pronunciation: E-lo heem*. God is the creator of the heavens and earth and all that is within it (Ps. 24:1). "In the beginning God created the heaven and the earth. . . And God said. Let us make man in our image, after our likeness. . . And God saw everything that [He] had made, and, behold, it was very good. . ." (Gen. 1:1, 26, 31).

Jehovah Jireh (The Lord Your Provider) – *pronunciation: Jehovah Ji-rah*. God provides for our every need and so much more. He asks us to "cast all [our] care upon Him for He careth for us" (1 Pet. 5:7). God is "the bread of life: and he that comes to [Him] shall never hunger; and he that believeth on Him shall never thirst" (Jn. 6:35).

Jehovah Mekoddishkem (The Lord who Sanctifies You) – *pronunciation: Jehovah Ma-kae-dish-kem*. We are washed, sanctified, and justified in the name of the Lord Jesus Christ, and by the Spirit of our God (Eph. 6:11). "What? know ye not that your body is the temple of the Holy Ghost which is in you, which ye have of God, and ye are not your own? For [we] are bought with a price: therefore glorify God in your body, and in your spirit, which are God's" (1 Cor. 6:19-20).

Jehovah Nisei (The Lord Your Battle Fighter) – *pronunciation: Jehovah Nee-see*. God is our battle fighter. Therefore, we must put on the whole armor of God and allow Him to use His armor to fight against the schemes and tactics of Satan. We must stand in the name of Jesus (Eph. 6:11-18), and He shall fight our battles. We must never give up. The Lord is strong and mighty in battle (Ps. 24:8). We are victorious through our Lord.

Jehovah Rohi (The Lord our Shepherd) – *pronunciation: Jehovah Row-high*. David wrote, "The LORD is my shepherd; I shall not want" (Ps. 23:1). Jesus stated "I am the good shepherd: the good shepherd giveth His life for the sheep . . . and know my sheep, and am known of mine. . . I lay down my life for the sheep" (Jn. 10:11, 14-15).

Jehovah Rapha (The Lord who Heals) – *pronunciation: Jehovah Raw-fee*. God can heal anything and every situation. Isaiah wrote, "But He was wounded for our transgressions, He was bruised for our iniquities: the chastisement of our peace was upon Him; and with His stripes we are healed" (Isa. 53:5). David wrote, "He healeth the broken in heart, and bindeth up their wounds" (Ps. 147:3).

Jehovah Sabaoth (The Lord of Hosts) – *pronunciation: Jehovah Se-ba-ot*. David stood with confidence knowing that God was the Lord of Hosts, and He would defeat the Philistine giant, Goliath. David replied to Goliath and said, "thou comest to me with a sword, and with a spear, and with a shield: but I come to thee in the name of the LORD of hosts, the God of the armies of Israel, whom thou has defied" (1 Sam. 17:45).

Jehovah Shalom (The Lord of Peace) – *pronunciation: Jehovah Sha-lome*. God is peace (Phil. 4:9). He is the peace of the world. He offers each one of us His peace "which passeth all understanding, [and] shall keep [our] hearts and minds through Christ Jesus" (Phil. 4:7). Jesus said, "Peace I leave with you, my peace I give unto you: not as the world giveth, give I unto you. Let not your heart be troubled, neither let it be afraid" (Jn. 14:27).

Jehovah Shammah (The Lord who is Always There) – *pronunciation: Jehovah Sha-mah*. You are God's child, and He is "with you always, even unto the end of the world" (Matt. 28:20). God, the Holy Spirit, resides within you (1 Cor. 6:19) and guides and comforts you. "[God] will never leave [you] nor forsake [you]" (Heb. 13:5).

Jehovah Tsidkenu (The Lord our Righteousness) – *pronunciation: Jehovah Tsid-kenu.* "And this is His name whereby He shall be called, THE LORD OUR RIGHTEOUSNESS" (Jer. 23:6). "The LORD is righteousness in all His ways, and holy in all His works" (Ps. 145:17). We are the righteousness of God through Jesus Christ (2 Cor. 5:21).

Jehovah Tsuri (The Lord our Rock) – *pronunciation: Jehovah T-soor.* "I will love thee, O LORD, my strength. The LORD is my rock, and my fortress, and my deliverer; my God, my strength, in whom I will trust; my buckler, and the horn of my salvation, and my high tower" (Ps. 18:1-2). Call upon the Lord and trust in Him. He is your rock. There is no rock like our God (1 Sam. 2:2).

Faith Affirmation: *The names of God have power.*

Prayer: Lord, I thank You for this day (Ps. 118:24), another day to call out Your name. You are "great and greatly to be praised" (Ps. 96:4). You have highly exalted Your son, our Lord and Savior, and You have given him a "name which is above every name [and] at the name of Jesus every knee shall bow, of things in heaven, and things in earth, and things under the earth; and that every tongue should confess that Jesus Christ is Lord, to the glory of God the Father" (Phil. 2:9-11).

Dear God Letter: Talk to God about your day. **The names of God** hold supreme power for your life and eternal salvation.

Dear God,

Date:
Day #:

ANOTHER DAY

In everything give thanks: for this is the will of God in Christ Jesus concerning you (1 Thess. 5:18).

L ord, I thank You for giving me another day to draw closer to You. I thank You for another day to:

Call on the name of Jesus Christ
Praise and Worship You
Exalt Your Name on High
Give Thanks unto You
Seek Your Kingdom and Righteousness
Have Faith and Only Believe
Bask in Your Mercy and Grace
Rest and Abide in You
Embrace Your Love
Smile and Laugh
Show my love for You
Enjoy Your Presence
Trust in You
Meditate on Your Word
Share Your Love
Labor in Your Name
Encourage Myself and Someone Else
Share My Testimony
Share My God-given Gifts
Bear the Fruit of the Spirit
Put on the Whole Armor of God
Spread the Gospel of Jesus Christ
Speak Life in the name of Jesus
Press toward the Mark for the Prize of the High Calling

Draw Closer to My Divine Purpose
Keep on Keeping On in the name of Jesus
LOVE YOU with all my heart and soul. . .

What are you thanking the Lord for today?

_____

_____

_____

Faith Affirmation: *Lord, I thank You for another day to draw closer to You.*

Prayer: Lord, I thank You for today (Ps. 118:24), another day to experience Your perfect love and draw closer to You. I bow down before You and worship You (Ps. 95:6). "Because Your lovingkindness is better than life, my lips shall praise thee" (Ps. 63:3). I thank You for filling me with You, the Holy Spirit, and allowing me to praise and thank You. You are a mighty and awesome God, and no matter the day or situation, I must give thanks to You. I love You, Lord.

Dear God Letter: Talk to God about your day. Remember to thank God for **another day to draw closer to Him**.

Dear God,

Date:
Day #:

FAITH IN GOD TESTIMONIES

And Jesus answering saith unto them, have faith in God (Mk. 11:22).

The Word of God states: "Have faith in God" (Mk. 11:22). "Now faith is the substance of things hoped for, the evidence of things not seen" (Heb.11:1). "But without faith, it is impossible to please [God] for [they] that cometh to God must believe that He is, and that He is a rewarder of them that diligently seek Him" (Heb. 11:6). Your faith in God, whether small or large, is pleasing unto God, and it will bring to pass those things that will bless you and glorify God.

How much faith do you have in God? And the disciples came to Jesus and said, "Why could we not cast him [the devil] out? And Jesus said unto them, Because of your unbelief: for verily I say unto you, If ye have faith as a grain of a mustard seed, ye shall say unto this mountain, Remove hence to yonder place; and it shall remove; and nothing shall be impossible unto you" (Matt. 17:19-20). Do you have faith in God that is the size of a mustard seed? If so,

God will honor your mustard seed faith.

God will honor your mustard seed faith, that small seed of faith that trusts the Lord to intervene and remove the impossible –that small grain of faith that acknowledges all things are possible to those who believe in God (Mk. 9:23), and these possibilities become our faith in God testimonies.

We have many "faith in God testimonies" but would like to share a testimony about our mother who we call mama. Our mama, who we love very much, has Alzheimer, a progressive and devastating brain disease that causes severe problems with memory, thinking and behavior, and it has no cure. As the disease has advanced, it has been extremely difficult to watch our mama go from a vibrant, outspoken woman who cared for herself and others to a woman who is dependent on her husband and children to provide her daily care. Each one of us is grieving the loss of our mama who raised, cared, and loved us. Yet, each one of us creates ways to experience the unseen beauty of our circumstances.

Our mama's circumstances seem to change each day. Those changes often create challenging moments for our mama and us. Yet, in the midst of those challenging moments, we also have experienced unforgettable blessings. A smile or chuckle that says, "I love you." A quick hip shake to one of her favorite songs that says, "I still got it." Or, a certain tone in her voice that brings back memories of the "good ole days" and offers us a glimpse of our courageous and wonderful mama. Those moments touch our hearts, strengthen our spirit, and allow us to feel the love of our mama. Those moments also confirm that our mama, the one who cared for us, comforted us, chastised us, protected us, and loved us with an unconditional mother's love, is being loved and protected by Jesus Christ, our Lord and Savior.

As we walk with our mama on this journey and experience the mysteries and devastations of Alzheimer that alter our lives and challenge our faith, we will trust in the Lord. We will hold on to our faith in God. Even though, at times, our faith may only be as a grain of a mustard seed, "our faith in God testimony" will declare that "our hope is in God, and no matter our circumstances, our mama, daddy, and family will be blessed in the name of Jesus Christ, and God will be glorified." Amen

Faith Affirmation: *I have faith in God.*

Prayer: Lord, I thank You for today (Ps. 118:24), another day to increase my faith and share my testimony. I choose to leave my burdens with You (1 Pet. 5:7). "In thy name shall [I] rejoice all day: and in thy righteousness shall [I] be exalted" (Ps. 89:16). O Lord, God of hosts, I trust and believe in You. I declare my faith in You no matter the situation or size of the obstacle.

Dear God Letter: Talk to God about your day. Thank Him for **your faith in God testimonies.**

Dear God,

Date:

Day #:

RELIEVING STRESS IN 20 SECONDS

Why art thou cast down, O my soul? And why art thou disquieted within me? Hope thou in God: for I shall yet praise Him, who is the health of my countenance, and my God (Ps. 42:11).

While waiting in line, the cover of a magazine sparked my attention. It sparked my attention because the title said, "How to Relieve Stress in 20 Seconds?" I immediately checked the index for the page number, and I anxiously anticipated finding the answer for relieving stress. As I quickly turned the pages, the Holy Spirit reminded me of the peace in praise. He reminded me that He could reduce my stress in 20 seconds. I took a deep breath and slowly released it. In my next breaths, I activated my 20 seconds of praise to God.

I thought Jesus, Jesus – 1000. Lord, I love You 1001. Hallelujah 1002. You are almighty 1003. I praise You for this moment 1004. I worship You 1005. Jesus, I glorify Your name 1006. God, You are awesome 1007. You are excellent 1008. I praise You for answering my prayers 1009. I thank You for being wonderful 1010. I praise You for being my every thing 1011. I praise You for Your strength and joy 1012. I praise You for loving and protecting my family 1013. I praise and thank You for eternal life 1014. I praise You for Your peace that surpasses all understanding 1015. I praise You for saving me 1016. You are my beginning and my end 1017. You are the author and finisher of my life 1018. You are God, and God alone 1019. There is none like You 1020.

Lord, I just can't stop praising Your name. I praise You for having a perfect plan for me. I praise and thank You for looking ahead and making provisions for me. I praise You for choosing me to do Your will. I praise You for a heart filled with love and gratitude. I praise You for always being with me and loving me with an everlasting love. Lord, You are my stress reliever, and I praise You!

The relief that you need is obtained in praise. Praising God opens your mind and heart to the goodness and power of God. Take the time to practice praising God daily. You can begin with twenty seconds. Twenty seconds may seem like a short moment of praise but several moments of praise during the day become minutes and minutes become hours. What if you practice praising and worshipping God when you aren't stressed? When you practice something you do it frequently; it becomes a habit.

A habit is something done often and hence, easily. Let your habit of praise and worship become an addiction. You need your praise and worship before you need anyone or anything. Praise and worship runs through your veins. It makes your adrenaline pump hard and fast. It provides you with peace and joy. You think about it most, if not all the time. You sleep with it. You eat with it. You bathe with it. You shop with it. Everywhere you go, it goes with you. Are you addicted to praise and worship? Are praise and worship something you do often and hence, easily? God inhabits the praises of His people (Ps. 22:3). Give God the highest praise, Hallelujah, Alleluia, Praise Jehovah!

Faith Affirmation: *My praise to God will relieve my stress.*

Prayer: Lord, I thank You for this day (Ps. 118:24). You are my wonderful Father. "I will praise thee, O Lord with my whole heart" (Ps. 9:1). I will sing praises unto Your name (Ps. 138). I will worship You and "praise thy name for thy lovingkindness and for thy truth: for thou has magnified thy word above all names" (Ps. 138:2). Lord, You are "great and greatly to be praised" (Ps. 96:4). "[Your] greatness is unsearchable" (Ps. 145:3). I am so grateful to have You in my life.

Dear God Letter: Talk to God about your day. If you want to **relieve your stress** and feel God's presence, praise Him in the name of Jesus. God inhabits the praises of His people (Ps. 22:3).

Dear God,

Date:
Day #:

THIS IS YOUR LIFE

For whoso findeth me findeth life, and shall obtain favor of the LORD
(Prov. 8:35).

I remember back in the 70's there was a show called *This Is Your Life*. A person would be invited as a guest on the show. Different people from the guest's life would tell stories about the person. The stories would range from childhood experiences all the way to current life events. Each individual would share special moments that they had experienced with the guest. It was always an emotional moment for the participant because each person had positively impacted their life in a significant way. Within about 60 minutes, the guest's life would be flashing right before their eyes. However, I noticed that the one guest they never invited was God, our Creator, and the author and finisher of our faith and lives (Heb. 12:2). As believers, we must remember this is our life, and it has been bought with a price, the blood of Jesus (1 Cor. 6:20). Our life belongs to God and nobody else; only we can live it with the guidance of the Holy Spirit.

Yes, this is your life and no matter what "all things work together for good to them that love God, to them who are the called according to His purpose" (Rom. 8:28). Take the time to remember key aspects of your life, the challenges and victories. Your life experiences have already connected to something in your present and future that will work out for your good. This is **your life** so just keep on living it in the name of Jesus. In Jesus, you have everything you need and much more. Keep God at the center of your life and you will continue to experience His love, power, and grace.

Keep God at the center of your life.

Faith Affirmation: *I am living my life for Jesus.*

195

Prayer: Lord, I thank You for today (Ps. 118:24) and all that You have done in my life and will do in my life. You are the potter and I am the clay (Isa. 64:8). I am Your vessel, and I have been created to do Your will. I will listen to Your voice, and I will obey You. You are my God, and I will trust You (Ps. 91:2). I delight myself in You. I commit my life to You, and I will continue to do Your will (Ps. 37:5). Lord, I love You.

Dear God Letter: Talk to God about your day. **This is your life.** No matter the season, allow the Holy Spirit to guide you through it in the name of Jesus.

Dear God,

God's Goodness And Beauty

Let all the earth fear the LORD: let all the inhabitants of the world stand in awe of Him. For He spake, and it was done; He commanded, and it stood fast (Ps. 33:8-9).

I went on an overnight bike trip with my daughter and her classmates. I had agreed to chaperone because I wanted to spend some time with them. When I arrived, I was quite uptight. I had worked really hard to get there and had gotten only about an hour of sleep. I had also had a pretty intense week. However, each day of that week I remained committed to praising God and trusting that I would obtain favor.

We started our biking in the morning. We biked for about two or three hours and then took a lunch break. During the bike ride, I prayed to God and praised His name. I prayed that God would help me relax and give me peace. After lunch, I noticed that I had peace. I could feel God's presence and His peace. This was only the beginning of my experience with God on this day.

God took me far beyond His peace that day; he also showed me His beauty and majesty. That evening, as I looked over the water toward the mountains, I was taken aback by God's beauty. The mountains that surrounded the campsite were tall and strong. As the sun began to set behind the mountains, its radiance caused the lake to shimmer and glisten. The girls played together by the lake and just laughed and laughed. In this moment, everything seemed to be in harmony – as one. This moment was just breathtaking and penetrated my heart. God reminded me that He had created the heavens and the earth. He reminded me that "the earth is the LORD's, and the fullness thereof; the world, and they that dwell therein" (Ps. 24:1). He had created beauty and in His beauty we find Him. In this precious moment with God,

> *God created beauty and in His beauty we find Him.*

197

I praised Him, talked with Him and worshiped Him. His beauty was upon me (Ps. 90:17), and it was humbling.

I had come to this island with my daughter to chaperon and enjoy this time with her and her classmates. God had brought me to the island so that He could gently remind me of His love, peace, beauty, and majesty. God is so awesome. Continue to seek God and He will continue to show you His goodness and offer you deliverance beyond your thoughts or imagination.

Faith Affirmation: *God's goodness offers deliverance beyond my thoughts or imagination.*

Prayer: Lord, I thank You for another day to behold Your goodness and beauty (Ps. 118:24). You are "great and greatly to be praised" (Ps. 96:4). I will take the time to bow down, praise, and worship You (Ps. 95:6). You are the Most High God (Ps. 97:9). "[You] gird me with strength, and maketh my way perfect" (Ps. 18:32). Your way is righteous and holy (1 Pet. 1:16). I love You, Lord.

Dear God Letter: Talk to God about your day. Thank God for **His goodness and majestic beauty** that offers you peace, joy, and deliverance.

Dear God,

Date:
Day #:

IT IS WHAT IT IS

And we know that all things work together for good, to them that love
God, to them who are the called according to His purpose . . .
(Rom. 8:28-30).

L ife just seems to happen, which includes the good and the not so good.
But it is what it is –life. Lately, I've been in several conversations
where people have stated, "It is what it is." Basically, you need to accept
the situation or circumstance as it is. Stop trying to make the situation into
something that it's not – It is what it is. You must stay focused on your
response to the situation. Are you able to keep a positive attitude? (Phil.
4:8). Are you able to stand in your faith? (Eph. 6:13-18). Are you able to
count it all joy? (Jas. 1:2-3).

As Christians, it is important for us to seek God so that He can show us
the situation for what it is. We will have a range of emotions as we experience life's trials and tribulations. At some
point, we will receive an emotional, mental,
physical and spiritual breakthrough in the
name of Jesus. This breakthrough will allow
us to come to a place where we can say "it is
what it is." Our "it is what it is" attitude will

It is what it is!

build our trust in God and draw us closer to Him. It will allow us to talk
with God and ask Him to give us wisdom, understanding, and guidance.
Our "it is what it is" attitude will provide us the opportunity to ask God to
show us how our attitude and position will benefit His people and us. Our
attitude will give us another opportunity to stand in the name of Jesus and
to believe.

A storm may be raging in your life. It is what it is, a storm that will
be calmed by God's peace. Your relationship has ended. It is what it is, a
relationship that God has allowed to end so that He can give you a new
beginning. You are not where you want to be in life. It is what it is. You are

exactly where God needs you to be. You have been diagnosed with breast cancer or some other type of illness. It is what it is, a diagnosis. It is God who has the power to render the final diagnosis and release His healing power. You are experiencing unspeakable love, joy, and peace. It is what it is, God's unconditional love, mercy, grace, and favor! Remember that "all things work together for good to them that love the Lord and are called according to his purpose. "For whom He did foreknow, He also did pre-destinate to be conformed to the image of his Son . . . Moreover whom He did predestinate, them He also called: and whom He called, them He also justified: and whom He justified, them he also glorified" (Rom. 8:28-30). Praise God. It is what it is. He is who He is – God.

Faith Affirmation: *It is what it is, and God has control of it.*

Prayer: Lord, I thank You for another day to rejoice and be glad (Ps. 118:24). I stepped into this day and was reminded that "it is what it is." You are who You are – the Most High God (Ps. 97:9). "How excellent is [Your] name in all the earth!" (Ps. 8:1). I count it a joy and privilege to know that where I am is no mystery to You. Through Your love, mercy, and power, You will work all situations together for my good (Rom. 8:28). I love You.

Dear God Letter: Talk to God about your day. Whatever you are experiencing or have experienced remember **it is what it is,** and God will render the end result for your good.

Dear God,

Date:
Day #:

ALWAYS IN THE SPIRIT

Praying always with all prayer and supplication in the Spirit. . .
(Eph. 6:18).

We all enjoy being in a place that is familiar and comfortable; yet, God also takes us to unfamiliar places that help us grow and draw closer to Him. The last time I was in an unfamiliar place, I prayed, fasted, cried, moaned, praised, worshiped, and talked with God. I told the LORD I didn't know what else to pray for or what else to do or not to do. God answered me and said, "Always praying in the Spirit" (Eph. 6:18). I immediately began to pray with the help of the Holy Spirit.

I knew my spirit was speaking to God, and what was spoken to God was unexplainable and incomprehensible. What a relief! My mind could not comprehend or even fathom the peace of the LORD in this unfamiliar place. "For he that speaketh in an unknown tongue speaketh not unto men, but unto God: for no man understands him; howbeit in the spirit he speaketh mysteries" (1 Cor. 14:2). In the Spirit, I found a new place. After having done all, I stood in this place (Eph. 6:13). My mind was quiet. My greatest consolation was I didn't know whom the Holy Spirit was praying for or what the Spirit was saying to the Lord, and I didn't care. I knew the Holy Spirit was speaking to the Father on my behalf. I would be victorious in the name of Jesus.

Now when my mind is racing, I pray in the Spirit. When my thoughts or feelings are anything but good, I seek God in the name of Jesus. After praying in the Spirit, I don't remember the unpleasant thoughts and if I do, I start praying again. You see I'm pressing for the goal of shifting my mindset and keeping my thoughts honest, just, pure, and lovely (Phil. 4:8). When I consistently pray in the Spirit, I practice shifting my mindset. With practice, my objective is to shift with ease. I wasn't consistently practicing in the unfamiliar place in my life. I am now.

As Christians, our daily mindset and actions impact the outcome of our daily victories. Therefore, we must put on God's whole armor, "Having your loins girt about with truth, and having on the breastplate of righteousness; and your feet shod with the preparation of the gospel of peace; above all, taking the shield of faith wherewith we shall be able to quench all the fiery darts of the wicked. And take the helmet of salvation, and the sword of the Spirit, which is the word of God" (Eph. 6:11-17). As we put on the armor, we must seek God for guidance; always praying in the Spirit (Eph. 6:18). God will bring to remembrance those scriptures and experiences that will strengthen us and allow us to proclaim the victory in the name of Jesus. In those unfamiliar, uncomfortable, and unusual places, God's armor will protect us and allow us to stand against the attacks of the devil (Eph. 6:11). I challenge you to put on God's armor and to be led by the Holy Spirit. You will be victorious!

Faith Affirmation: *I will pray in the Spirit.*

Prayer: Lord, I thank You for this Spirit-filled day (Ps. 118:24). You are Lord, "and there is none else, there is no God beside [You]" (Isa. 45:5). I will lift up my hands and bless You (Ps. 134). I will "[put on] the whole armor of God, that [I] may be able to withstand in the evil day" (Eph. 6:13) and fulfill my divine purpose. I will pray "always with all prayer and supplication in the Spirit" (Eph. 6:18).

Dear God Letter: Talk to God about your day. Remember to always **pray in the Spirit** and stand in the name of Jesus.

Dear God,

Date:
Day #:

CALMNESS AND PEACE IN GOD

*Be still, and know that I am God: I will be exalted among the heathen,
I will be exalted in the earth (Ps. 46:10).*

We must be still and know that He is God. (Ps. 46:10). We must also welcome the calmness and peace of the Father to dwell in our hearts (Col. 3:15-17). The indwelling of the Lord, the Holy Spirit, allows us to rest in His perfect peace (Phil. 4:7). The indwelling of God enables us to do His will. The indwelling of the Holy Spirit offers us hope and expectancy, a heart of praise and worship, an intimate relationship with our Father and a breakthrough in every area of our lives.

We do not have to be moved like the Israelites and become so afraid that we turn our attention away from our Savior. We must not fear but "stand still, and see the salvation of the Lord" (Ex. 14:13). We will remind our adversaries that our Lord will fight for us, and we will hold our peace (Ex. 14:14). We will rest in the Lord and wait patiently for Him (Ps. 37:7). He will exalt us to inherit the land and be victorious (Ps. 37:34). We must "keep [our] feet shod with the preparation of the gospel of peace; above all, taking the shield of faith, wherewith [we] shall be able to quench all the fiery darts of the wicked" (Eph. 6:15-16).

Whatever we do as children of God, we must strive to maintain our calmness and peace in God (Phil. 4:7). Our calmness and peace in God are evidence that we have surrendered our will unto the Lord. Our calmness and peace are a great witness to others. They allow us to stand firm in God, even in the midst of frustration, anger, confusion, hurt or fear. We don't have to be terrified by our enemy the devil or his weapons (2 Tim. 1:7). We must "stand fast in one Spirit, with one mind striving together for the faith of the gospel" (Phil. 1:27). We will wait with expectancy knowing that God is working and speaking in our stillness. He will answer and work out everything for our good.

203

Take the time to be still and acknowledge God (Ps. 46:10). He offers calmness and peace to all those who will receive it. God's peace and calmness is mighty and will pull down strongholds and offer you deliverance and rest. Will you press for your peace and calmness? Will you walk in your peace and calmness with us? Come on. God is waiting for you.

Faith Affirmation: *I will rest in God's peace and calmness.*

Prayer: Lord, I thank You for another day to acknowledge how great You are in my life (Ps. 118:24). You alone are worthy to be praised (Ps. 113). "[You] shall cover [me] with Your feathers, and under [Your] wings shalt [I] trust: [Your] truth shall be [my] shield and buckler. . ." (Ps. 91:4). I will be still and acknowledge You are God, my Lord and Savior. In my stillness, I will rest in Your love, hope, and peace.

Dear God Letter: Talk to God about your day. Your **calmness and peace come from trusting the Lord**.

Dear God,

Date:
Day #:

LAUGHTER

A merry heart doeth good like a medicine: but a broken spirit drieth the bones (Prov. 17:22).

I love to laugh. I think it's just a part of my wiring. Do you like to laugh? Or, do you love to laugh? The Word says, "a merry heart doeth good like a medicine" (Prov. 17:22). Laughter is one of the manifestations of a merry heart, and therefore good like medicine. Laughter medicine will keep your heart from failing. It will help soothe the issues of life that impact the heart. It will also help relieve stress and keep your circumstances in perspective.

I laugh when I watch cartoons. I laugh when folks tell good and bad jokes. I laugh when I tell jokes, make funny comments or faces. I laugh when my children say, "Mom, not to be mean or anything but that isn't funny." I even laugh sometimes when I probably shouldn't. I remember the time that my husband smashed his finger, and I just busted out laughing. I wasn't laughing about him getting hurt – no really I wasn't. I was laughing at all the faces and noises that he was making.

One day my sister and I were on the telephone talking about a family matter and began to fuss, which is something that we don't do very often. After we hung up, I thought this is not right. Satan is a lie. I called her back and made a funny noise on the phone and said, "This is crazy!" We just started cracking up.

Several years ago, our younger sister was diagnosed with breast cancer and chose to take chemotherapy as a way to fight that cancer. She and my family diligently sought God for her healing, and it is by His stripes she is healed (Isa. 53:5). During the time she was going to chemotherapy, we went out to lunch. We decided to wear wigs to lunch to support our sister who had lost her hair due to the chemotherapy treatments. While sitting at the table, I decided to switch my "sexy" wig around every time the waiter came to serve us. I switched it to the side, the back, and the other side and back to the front. It looked ridiculous. We watched the waiter to see if he could keep his composure. He tried really hard. We laughed so hard that our stomachs and heads ached. Every time I think about that day, I just smile and start laughing. Laughter is like medicine for the heart.

I remember the time I waged war on the squirrels that were living in my attic. Those squirrels waged war back and took my big black underwear out of the go out bag that was on my porch and hung them up in the neighbor's large cherry tree. I looked out my window and saw my underwear and almost passed out. Oh, that incident was hilarious!

Did I tell you about the time my 3-year-old daughter called me a jackass? Well, she didn't exactly call me a jackass. One day she got upset with me and yelled from her room, "Mom, you're a donkey like Eeyore" – that's close enough to calling me a jackass. Or, the time my 4-year-old son called my niece an inappropriate name and I told him no name-calling. He said without missing a beat, "Mom, I'm not calling names; I'm speaking Spanish." Yeah, right. He actually thought to say that. I could go on and on. I have so many moments in my life that I can think about and just burst out laughing. I bet you do too.

Laughter medicine will keep your heart from failing.

God has given you the ability to laugh, so laugh. You can laugh in the good times as well as the bad. Sometimes life just seems so hard or out of control and that's when you really have to pause for a moment and laugh. You have to reach into your heart and pull out a joke, a funny thought or humorous incident. Go ahead and laugh; there is a lot of stuff in this life that's funny. Take the time to think about different situations in your life that have made you laugh and laugh all over again. Take the time to open up your heart to God and allow Him to bring you more laughter. After all, laughter is a manifestation of a merry heart and therefore "doeth good like a medicine" (Prov. 17:22).

Faith Affirmation: *I will laugh; it's good medicine for my heart.*

Prayer: Father, I thank You for another day to laugh and be glad (Ps. 118:24). I will praise You with all my heart (Ps. 9:1). I will sing praises unto You from the depth of my soul (Ps. 92:1). I will rejoice with You in all circumstances (Phil. 4:4). I will embrace life and laugh, laugh, and laugh some more. I will allow my laughter to be medicine for my heart (Prov. 17:22).

Dear God Letter: Talk to God about your day. Remember, God loves to hear you laugh. **Laughter is good for your heart.**

Dear God,

GOD FORGIVES

*If we confess our sins, He is faithful and just to forgive us of our sins,
and cleanse us from all unrighteousness (1Jn. 1:9).*

D o you know that God forgives? Do you really know that God forgives and requests that you accept His forgiveness? Forgiveness is a gift from God that should be received with an open heart. His Word says that "if [you] confess [your] sins He is faithful and just to forgive [you] of [your] sins and to cleanse [you]" (1 Jn. 1:9). So, not only does He offer the gift of forgiveness, He also offers to cleanse you (wash, purify, clean, free us) from our unrighteousness (sin). You don't have to return to that sin again. Your sin has been cleansed (washed) away by the blood of the Lamb, Jesus Christ.

God offers the gift of forgiveness to all who ask for His forgiveness. I once heard someone say that their sin was too horrible for God to forgive. Another person stated, "I've been doing this so long; He won't forgive me?" Someone else said, "I've taken this to Him before; He won't forgive me again." God's answer to their concerns, "You are my child and I love you with an everlasting love. 'If you

God Forgives

confess your sins, I am faithful and just to forgive you of your sins, and to cleanse you from all unrighteousness'" (1 Jn. 1:9). It's important for you to remember that there is no new sin under the sun (Eccles. 1:9). There is nothing that is too hard or impossible for God (Jer. 32:27; Matt. 19:26).

The Bible is filled with life stories of people sinning against God and then seeking His forgiveness; and He did forgive them. His Word says, "We have all sinned and come short of the glory of God" (Rom. 3:23). Yet, if anyone confesses their sin; they shall receive the gift of forgiveness. God loves you and knows that you are not perfect; only He is perfect. God is

209

full of "compassion, and gracious, long suffering, and plenteous in mercy and truth" (Ps. 86:15) and ready always to forgive you (Ps. 86:5).

God knows that you will face challenges and you will sin against Him. Through it all, He wants you to remember that He loves you, and He is a forgiving God. Take the time today to ask God for forgiveness and to accept His gift of forgiveness. Let His gift sink deep down into your heart and soul freeing you to walk in His love and liberty.

Faith Affirmation: Lord, I thank You for forgiving me.

Prayer: Lord, I thank You for this day. This is the day that You have made and I will rejoice and be glad in it (Ps. 118:24). You are my Lord and Savior and You love me. You are "full of compassion, and gracious, long suffering, and plenteous in mercy and truth" (Ps. 86:15), and You are always ready to forgive (Ps. 86:5). I confess my sin and believe that You will forgive me and cleanse me of my unrighteousness. I receive Your love and gift of forgiveness.

Dear God Letter: Talk to God about your day. **Confess your sins and ask God for forgiveness.** He is faithful and just to forgive.

Dear God,

AM I STILL ON THE THRONE?

The Lord hath prepared His throne in the heavens; and His kingdom ruleth over all (Ps. 103:19).

A m I still on the throne? Of course, I AM is still on the throne, no matter what. God the Father, God the Son, and God the Holy Spirit will forever be on the throne. As we go through the seasons in our lives, God is constantly reminding us that He is still on His throne. He doesn't remind us because we wonder or think that He is not. He reminds us because no matter what report we may get, what situation may come up, what may have been accomplished or not accomplished, He remains on His throne. He is the only constant in our life. He's always available. He won't change (Heb. 13:8). He won't leave nor forsake us (Heb. 13:5). He won't fail us. His love is everlasting (Jer. 31:3).

He is such an awesome God! Where you go, His feet are there or His feet have already been! Because the earth is His footstool, He has rested His feet in every place you have gone and will go. His Word tells you that "heaven is [His] throne, and the earth is [His] footstool" (Isa. 66:1). His throne is available to you any time of day and any moment of the night. You can rest at His feet in perfect peace.

No matter how your life appears to be going or not going, His throne brings His Word to your remembrance. At God's throne, His Son, Jesus, "maketh intercession for [you] according to the will of God" (Rom. 8:27). His angels excel in strength, do His commandments, and hearken unto the voice of His Word (Ps. 103:20). No matter how long His answer may seem to take and no matter what weapon is formed, "[His Word] shall not return unto Him void, but it shall accomplish that which [He] pleases, and it shall prosper in the thing whereto [He] sent it" (Isa. 55:11). Amen

How often do you go to God's throne and spend time at His feet? Do you exercise your right as a child, a priest, a prince or princess to spend time at His throne and at His feet? What or who prevents you from spending time at His feet? Come to God's throne and allow Him to be I AM in your life.

Faith Affirmation: *I AM is on the throne watching over me.*

Prayer: Lord, I thank You for today (Ps. 118:24). "O LORD, how great are thy works! And thy thoughts are very deep" (Ps. 92:5). I will bless You Lord. I will bless You with all that is within me (Ps. 103:1-2). Father, You reign with all majesty and strength (Ps. 93:1). "[Your] throne is established of old; [You] art from everlasting" (Ps. 93:2) and will forever remain on Your throne.

Dear God Letter: Talk to God about your day. Remember **I AM is still on His throne** full of power and majesty. He is available to you any moment of the day or night.

Dear God,

THE KNITTING OF TWO SOULS

Then Jonathan and David made a covenant, because he loved him as his own soul (1 Sam. 18:3).

J onathan and David had a relationship knitted together by love –God's love. It was an unexpected relationship, but it was given to them as a gift from God. A relationship that has shed light on God's covenant and love for His children. David and Jonathan's relationship, commitment and love for each other were integral to their destiny. "And it came to pass, when [David] had made an end of speaking [with] Saul, that the soul of Jonathan was knit with the soul of David, and Jonathan loved him as his own soul" (1 Sam. 18:1). Jonathan and David loved each other with an unexplainable love – a love that penetrated their heart and soul – a love that wove their hearts together. It was impossible to see where Jonathan and David's love began or ended or explain its depth and power. God had intervened and knitted their souls together.

God allowed His love to show through the love between Jonathan and David. God ordained that their soul, their existence and destiny would be knitted together, and He established a covenant relationship between them. This covenant relationship allowed David and Jonathan to trust each other in the hardest of times, even though it meant Jonathan would have to betray his father to save David's life.

Jonathan assisted David with keeping one step ahead of his father as Saul pursued David. Jonathan provided David with information that allowed him to escape from Saul's death trap (1 Sam. 20). David knew that Jonathan was risking his own life to save his life. David wanted no harm to come to Jonathan but could do nothing to help him. There were no words to say except God had intervened and knitted their souls together.

With Jonathan's assistance, David escaped from Saul's many attacks against his life. However, Jonathan was eventually killed on the battlefield along with his father, and upon hearing of the death of Saul and Jonathan,

David grieved. He cried ". . . I am distressed for thee, my brother Jonathan: very pleasant hast thou been unto me: thy love to me was wonderful, passing the love of women" (2 Sam. 1:26).

In later years, out of his love for Jonathan, David sought to find out if there were any family members left of the house of Saul, so that he could show kindness for Jonathan's sake (2 Sam. 9). Jonathan had a son, Mephibosheth, who was heir to the throne of Israel and had hidden for fear of being killed by King David. David would find Mephibosheth, and he would honor his love for Jonathan and set his son in his rightful royal place among men. Who would have thought that their covenant would exceed beyond Jonathan's death? Nobody but God.

Once we accept Christ into our lives, we accept God's covenant of love, which is everlasting to everlasting. His covenant required He clothe Himself in flesh in the form of Jesus Christ and be crucified on the cross so that we would be reconciled back to Him (Phil. 2:5-11): A covenant filled with His love, power, mercy, and grace; A covenant sealed with the blood of Jesus and maintained by God, the Holy Spirit (Titus 3:4-7). God's love goes beyond what we can conceive, and there is no beginning or ending for God is love (1 Jn. 4:8).

Faith Affirmation: *God has a covenant relationship with me.*

Prayer: Lord, this is the day that You have made and allowed me to experience Your lovingkindness (Ps. 63:3). I thank You for the opportunity to rejoice and be glad in it (Ps. 118:24). Father, I thank You for sending Jesus Christ to lay down His life so that I would not perish but have everlasting life (Jn. 3:16). It is Your love, power, and grace that sustain me in a covenant relationship with You. I love You.

Dear God Letter: Talk to God about your day. **God has knitted your soul to His**, and He has established a covenant relationship with you.

Dear God,

Date:
Day #:

HOPE THOU IN GOD

And now, Lord, what wait I for? My hope is in thee (Ps. 39:7).

I n one day, Job, a man of God, was informed that his children had been killed; his servants were slain, and his sheep were consumed by fire. Job ripped his robe, shaved his head, and fell down upon the ground and worshiped the Lord (Job 1:20). Job spoke from a heart of sadness, love, and hope in the Lord, "Naked came I out of my mother's womb, and naked shall I return thither: the LORD gave, and the LORD hath taken away; blessed be the name of the LORD" (Job 1:21). Job did not sin against the Lord (Job 1:22).

After this tragic day, Satan again tried to destroy Job and convince him to curse God. Satan covered Job with sores from the sole of his foot to the top of his head (Job 2:7). Surely with the loss of his children, servants, wealth and now the agonizing sores, Job would lose hope in the Lord and curse Him. Job's wife even suggested that Job curse God, and die (Job 2:9). Job spoke from his heart of hope unto his wife, "Thou speakest as one of the foolish women speaketh. What? Shall we receive good at the hand of God, and shall we not receive evil? In all this did not Job sin with his lips" (Job 2:10). Why? Job's hope (utmost confidence) was in the Lord.

> *We must maintain our hope and utmost confidence in the Lord.*

As we are tested and tried in life, each one of us must maintain our hope, our utmost confidence in the Lord, knowing that He is who He says He is. He is the Messiah, the only begotten Son of God (Jn. 3:16). He is "the way, the truth, and the life: and no [one] cometh to the Father, but by [Jesus]" (Jn. 14:6). He is I AM THAT I AM (Ex. 3:14). He "hath begun a good work in [us] and will perform it until the day of Jesus Christ" (Phil.

217

1:6). He will always be with us "even until the end of the world" (Matt. 28:20). "God is love" (1 Jn. 4:8), and He loves us (1 Jn. 4:10).

No matter the adversity, we must rest in God's love knowing that "all things work together for good to them that love God, to them who are the called according to His purpose" (Rom. 8:28). It is God who "will go before [us] and make the crooked places straight" (Isa. 45:2). He is Lord. No matter the situation, circumstance or condition, keep your hope in the Lord, Elohim, the One who made the earth, stretched out the heavens, created you, and offers you His unconditional love. "Be of good courage, and He shall strengthen your heart, all ye that hope in the Lord" (Ps. 31:24).

Paul wrote, "Nay, in all things we are more than conquerors through Him that loved us. For I am persuaded, that neither death, nor life, nor angels, nor principalities, nor powers, nor things present, nor things to come, nor height, nor depth, nor any other creature, shall be able to separate us from the love of God, which is in Christ Jesus our Lord" (Rom. 8:37-39). He is "Christ in you, the hope of glory" (Col. 1:27) and the hope of your salvation.

Faith Affirmation: *My hope is in the Lord.*

Prayer: Lord, I thank You for another day full of Your hope, joy and glory (Ps. 118:4). Lord, You are "good [and Your] mercy endureth forever" (Ps. 136:1). You are I AM THAT I AM in my life (Ex. 3:14). It is You who dwells within me (1 Cor. 3:16). You "make the crooked places straight" (Isa. 45:2). You protect me against my enemies (Ps. 27). Lord, my hope will always be in You (Ps. 39:7).

Dear God Letter: Talk to God about your day. Remember to **put your hope in God**. "He is Christ in you, the hope of glory" (Col. 1:26).

Dear God,

Date:

Day #:

FRUIT INSPECTION

*Now the works of the flesh are manifest, which are these; Adultery, forni-
cation, uncleanness, [lustfulness], idolatry, witchcraft, hatred, [conten-
tion], [jealousy], wrath, strife, [dissensions], heresies, envyings, murders,
drunkenness, [excessiveness], and such like . . . But the fruit of the Spirit
is love, joy, peace, [patience], gentleness, goodness, faith, meekness,
[self-control]: against such there is no law (Gal. 5:19-23).*

I n my backyard, we have two plum trees. Some of our neighbors and
friends have plum, apple, pear, peach, apricot, and/or orange trees. Each
year during the spring and summer, those trees produce plenty of fruit.
Many people look forward to this time of the year. They have many great
plans for the fruit. Some sell the fruit while others enjoy a fresh piece of
fruit and others make dessert or some other type of food. One of my friends
makes apple and plum jelly. My mom would make apple pies, apple sauce,
apple cake, peach cobbler – so, so good – and pear sauce. For a spring
family brunch, my mother would fry up some hot chicken; make home-
made biscuits, pear sauce, rice and rich brown creamy gravy. Mmm, Mmm
good! My mother is a great cook. Alright, I got off track thinking about
what my mother could do with some fresh fruit and all the great memories
that come along with eating her great cooking. Okay, back to the message.
Apple trees produce apples. Plum trees plums. Peach trees produce peaches
and pear trees produce pears. Each tree, if cared for correctly, will produce
an abundance of its designated fruit.

As Christians, we are similar to the fruit trees, but definitely more than
fruit trees. Upon accepting Christ into our lives, God plants Himself, the
Holy Spirit, inside of us (1 Cor. 3:16). He requests that we seek Him for
nourishment and growth. He requires that we seek Him so that we can
become the (tree) person that He has called us to become (Jer. 1:5; 1 Thess.
5:24). As we grow in Christ, we manifest the fruit of the Spirit – love,
joy, peace, faith, meekness, long suffering, gentleness, and goodness (Gal.

5:22-23), which is evidence that our roots are planted in God and are being nourished by God the Holy Spirit.

Christians bear many types of fruit, not just one fruit. This fruit benefits our walk as well as it benefits the lives of others. Folks see the fruit that we bear and want to bear the same fruit, which requires that they accept Jesus Christ as their personal savior and walk with Him according to His will. We have the opportunity to look at our fruit and ask God to show us how to manifest all the fruit of the Spirit. This requires us to seek God, repent, and allow Him to care for us. It is God's care that allows us to bear more spiritual fruit and different types of His fruit.

Have you inspected your fruit lately? Have you asked God to inspect your fruit? What type of fruit is coming from your tree? Is it the fruit of the Spirit or the fruit of the flesh? Is your fruit pleasing unto God? Have you asked God to show you how to bear more and/or different fruits of the Spirit? Have you asked God to show you how to use the fruits of the Spirit? Are you allowing your fruit to edify and build up you and the believer? Check your fruit today; it offers so many opportunities and possibilities — joy pie, peace cobbler, meekness soup, faith pudding, temperance syrup, gentleness jam, and goodness sauce.

Faith Affirmation: *I will bear the fruit of the Spirit.*

Prayer: Lord, I thank You for today (Ps. 118:24), another day to bear Your fruit. You are "great and greatly to be praised" (Ps. 96:4). I will forever praise and worship You (Ps. 95:1-6). It is my desire to live and walk in the Spirit (Gal. 5:25), to do Your will, and to daily produce the fruit of the Spirit (Gal. 6:8). I love You, Lord.

Dear God Letter: Talk to God about your day. Put your fruit before the Lord and ask Him to complete a **fruit inspection**. You will be amazed at what you find out.

Dear God,

Date:
Day #:

WELL, WHAT HAD HAPPENED WAS

♡♡

Avoid it, pass not by it, turn from it and pass away (Prov. 4:15).

Well, what had happened was. There was a woman who was struggling with gossiping so she decided to stay away from her group of friends that gossiped. Right. But one day she decided she would just meet with them after work. They all got together and the gossiping began. She felt uncomfortable but didn't leave. She decided that she would listen and not gossip. After a while, she excused herself to go to the restroom. Right. Upon returning to the table, she overheard her "friends" gossiping about her. She was outdone. Her feelings were hurt, and what they were saying was not true. The Lord reminded her that He had called her away from gossiping and those individuals. He also reminded her that gossip hurts. She had been called to speak those words that are kind, right, uplifting and just.

Well, what had happened was. A woman had sought the Lord on a concern related to fantasies that were impacting her concentration. Right. There was this fine male at work who she would flirt with just a little, but it wasn't anything that she couldn't handle. Right. Well, one day Mr. Goodbar asked her to lunch and she decided to go. The next week or so he asked her to dinner. To make a long "well, what had happened was" story short, the next thing she knew she was having sex with Mr. Goodbar. Oh, it was good to the flesh, but harmful to her spirit. The Lord spoke to her. He reminded her how much He loved her. He told her that the desires of her heart would be fulfilled by the man that He had called to love her. She repented and ran into the arms of the Lord. He restored her to her rightful place with Him.

Well, what had happened was. A woman accepted Christ into her life and was a strong warrior for the Lord. She read the Word, prayed, and worshiped.

> *Well, what had happened was.*

She spread the Good News of Jesus Christ. Right. Then she got sick and couldn't see her way to recovery. She became angry with God. How could He allow this to happen? She was a child of God. She stopped seeking God. She stopped reading the Word and spreading the Good News of Jesus Christ. She became depressed. One late night, the Lord woke her up and reminded her that great is His mercies toward her (Ps. 103:11). He reminded her that He has the power to heal (Isa. 53:5). He has power over life and death (Jn. 11:25; Matt. 28:18). He reminded her that He loves her more than she could think, feel or imagine. She had much to be thankful for, if only she would stop and experience his lovingkindness. The woman felt God's loving presence and wept. In that moment, she allowed her heart to be healed.

We all have a "Well, what had happened was" story. Right? But remember we must continue to avoid, cast down and resist those temptations that are placed before us to destroy our walk with God. If for some reason we are unable to resist a temptation, we can seek God and ask Him for forgiveness (1 Jn. 1:9). He will make our situation work together for our good (Rom. 8:28). We will be able to say, well, what had happened was, I called on the name of the Lord, a very present help in the time of trouble, and He delivered me (Ps. 46:1).

Faith Affirmation: *I will call on the name of the Lord. He is a very present help.*

Prayer: Lord, it is because of You that I was able to rejoice today (Ps. 118:24). You are "great and greatly to be praised" (Ps. 96:4). I will praise You with my whole heart (Ps. 9:1). "It is [You, Oh Lord], that girdeth me with strength, and make my way perfect" (Ps. 18:32). No matter the situation, I will seek You; for great is Your mercy and lovingkindness toward me (Ps. 63:3). You are with me always (1Jn. 4:13) and Your love for me is everlasting (Jer. 31:3).

Dear God Letter: Talk to God about your day. We all have a **well, what had happened was story**. Thank God for intervening and working the situation out for your good.

Dear God,

Date:
Day #:

MARKED TERRITORY

The earth is the LORD's, and the fulness thereof; the world, and they that dwell therein (Ps. 24:1).

I have been told bears claw at trees and leave their claw marks as a sign that they have been there. Lions fight to ensure that the pride recognizes who leads the pride. Dogs express themselves on trees or fire hydrants that signify they have been there. On the job, people put up door plaques that identify their titles and office space. Other folks put up fences to mark their territory or property. A person may snuggle up a little extra with their mate to let everyone know that they are together. Some married folks wear wedding rings to show their love and commitment, but also to confirm that this person is taken, not available, married with three kids (smile) – alright, you get the point.

A friend reminded me that we also have "marked territory" for Christ. Therefore, we must remain sober and vigilant, seeking God for strength and direction, ministering to God's people, and spreading the Good News of Jesus Christ in God's marked territory, which is the world and the fullness thereof (Ps. 24:1). We must remain sober and vigilant because our adversary the devil comes as a roaring lion, walking about seeking to destroy us (1 Pet. 5:8). His roar produces fear and can often cause God's people to retreat or stop doing God's will. It can cause us to give up our marked territory – that dream, idea, witness, prayer, or relationship – which often leaves us feeling defeated. It also leads us into disobedience with God. Remember the devil's goal is to steal, kill, and destroy your life (Jn. 10:10).

God came that you might have life and have it more abundantly (Jn. 10:10). Remember that you are filled with the Holy Spirit, God Himself (1 Cor. 3:16). You have been marked and called by God. Before you were formed in your mother's womb, He marked and called you (Jer. 1:5). You are fearfully and wonderfully made by God (Ps. 139:14) and created in His

229

own image and likeness (Gen. 1:26). He plans to complete a good work in you (Phil. 1:6).

The Lord marked His territory when He created the heavens and earth and all that is within it (Ps. 24:1). The roaring lion, our adversary the devil, would like you to believe that God has not marked you nor purposed and called you (Jer. 1:5; Phil. 1:6). He would like for you not to experience God's goodness, love, peace, joy, mercy, and favor. He would like for you not to receive the prize of the high calling, that you would "dwell in the house of the Lord all the days of [your] life, to behold the beauty of the LORD, and to inquire in His temple" (Ps. 27:4).

You have been marked and called by God.

Resist the devil by rebuking him in the name of Jesus and speaking the word of the Lord. Resist the devil through your trust and faith in God and commitment to having victorious thoughts and a positive attitude. "Submit yourselves therefore to God. Resist the devil, and he will flee from [you]" (Jas. 4:7). You are a part of God's marked territory. How so, He lives within you.

Do you know, that you know, that you know, that you are a child of God? (1 Jn. 4:4). Do you know that you have been called by God and filled with the Holy Spirit, God Himself? (1 Cor. 3:16). Do you know that God comforts, guides, and protects you? (2 Cor. 1:3-4). Do you know that God is with you until the ends of the world? (Matt. 28:20). Do you know that God loves you with an unconditional love? (Jn. 3:16). Do you know that God has numbered the hairs on your head? (Matt. 10:30). Do you also know that if His eye is on the sparrow then surely He watches over you? (Matt. 10:31). Remain sober and vigilant in the name of Jesus Christ, seeking always to do His will. Trust and delight in the Lord and He shall give you the desires of your heart (Ps. 37:3-4).

Faith Affirmation: *I will be sober and vigilant in the name of Jesus.*

Prayer: Lord, I thank You for providing me with another day to rejoice in You (Ps. 118:24). I will forever bless Your righteous and holy name (Ps. 99:3). I thank You that I have been marked by You. I belong to You and will do Your will. I will be sober and vigilant in the name of Jesus. I will go out and mark Your territory by spreading the gospel of Jesus Christ (Matt. 28:19) and ministering to Your people.

Dear God Letter: Talk to God about your day. Remember to be sober and vigilant with the **marked territory** God has given to you.

Dear God,

Date:
Day #:

IT'S JUST THAT SIMPLE

That if thou shalt confess with thy mouth the Lord Jesus, and shalt believe in thine heart that God hath raised him from the dead, thou shall be saved. . . (Rom. 10:9-10).

J esus Christ is the only begotten Son of God (Jn. 3:16). And Jesus asked Simon Peter, "But whom do ye say that I am? And Simon Peter answered and said, Thou art the Christ, the Son of the living God" (Matt. 16:15-16). In that moment, Peter spoke forth what he believed and what was revealed to him by God, the Father.

Yes, if you confess the Lord Jesus Christ, and believe God raised Him from the dead, you shall be saved (Rom. 10:9). Salvation is a gift from God (Eph. 2:8-9). You shall be filled with God the Holy Spirit and be sealed unto the day of redemption (Eph. 4:30) and "dwell in the house of the Lord, all the days of your life, to behold the beauty of the Lord and to inquire in His temple" (Ps. 27:4). If you trust in the Lord, you will experience His love, joy, mercy, and grace. "Trust in the Lord . . . and "delight thyself also in the Lord; and He shall give [you] the desires of [your] heart" (Ps. 37:3-4).

Confess the name of Jesus Christ (Rom. 10:9). "Stand fast in the liberty wherewith Christ hath set you free, and be not entangled again with the yoke of bondage" (Gal. 5:1). "Now the Lord is that Spirit: and where the Spirit of the Lord is, there is liberty" (2 Cor. 3:17). Be led by the Spirit and you shall bear the fruit of the Spirit which is love, joy, peace, long suffering, gentleness, goodness, faith, meekness, and temperance (Gal. 5:22). Walk and live in the Spirit (Gal. 5:25), and ye shall inherit the kingdom of God. No really, it's just that simple. He's waiting for you to come to Him.

Faith Affirmation: *I believe with my heart and confess with my mouth that Jesus Christ is Lord.*

Prayer: Lord, I thank You for giving me another day to live and exalt You (Ps. 118:24; Ps. 145:2). "How excellent is [Your] name in all the earth" (Ps. 8:1). I confess that "thou art Christ, the Son of the living God" (Matt. 16:15-16). It is by Your grace that I am saved. It is Your gift of love that You freely give to me. (Eph. 2:8-9).

Dear God Letter: Talk to God about your day. Confess Jesus Christ as your Lord and Savior and you shall be saved. **It's just that simple.**

Dear God,

WE GREW UP

When I was a child I spake as a child, I understood as a child, I thought as a child: but when I became man, I put away childish things (1 Cor. 13:11).

We grew up as kids
We were born a child of God
We grew up as kids; we lived a childhood filled with good and bad times
God held us and covered us with His love, mercy, and grace
He knocked, giving us an opportunity to answer His call
Some answered and accepted the salvation of God
While others thought they would just wait for another day.

We grew up as kids with the hurts of childhood, a deep laughter, and a zeal for life
We grew up as friends, cousins, neighbors, brothers, and sisters
We grew up as kids and then became teenagers
Each believing that we could reach the stars
Each believing that we would excel
God held us and covered us with His love, mercy, and grace
He knocked, giving us an opportunity to answer His call
Some answered and accepted the salvation of God
While others thought they would just wait for another day.

We grew up into adults trying to handle life
We knew love, joy, disappointment, hardships, sickness, promotions, finances, children, singleness, marriage, divorce, and much, much more
God held us and covered us with His love, mercy, and grace
He knocked, giving us an opportunity to answer His call
Some answered and accepted the salvation of God
While others thought they would just wait for another day.

God continues to knock at the heart of His children

Those who have not answered God's call can pray this heartfelt prayer: Lord, come into my life; I confess Jesus Christ as my Lord and Savior (Rom. 10:9)

Those who have answered His call can rejoice knowing that they will meet Him in heaven to behold His beauty (Ps. 27:4) and hear our Lord and Savior say, "Well done good and faithful [child], well done"(Matt. 25:21).

Faith Affirmation: *God, You are my Lord and Savior.*

Prayer: Lord, I thank You for today (Ps. 118:24). "Every day will I bless thee; and I will praise thy name forever and ever" (Ps. 145:2). You are my Creator, Lord and Savior. "When I was a child I spake as a child, I understood as a child, I thought as a child: [but when I accepted You in my life], I put away childish things" (1 Cor. 13:11) and focused on loving and pleasing You. Lord, I thank You for loving me and giving me the gift of eternal life (Eph. 2:8-9).

Dear God Letter: Talk to God about your day. Remember, **as you grow in Christ,** you will mature in God.

Dear God,

COME OUT, COME OUT, WHEREVER YOU ARE

O God, thou knowest my foolishness; and my sins are not hid from thee (Ps. 69:5).

When I was a child, we used to play a game called Hide and Go Seek. There was a seeker who would cover their eyes and count to ten. While the seeker was counting, the hiders would run and find a hiding place. Once the seeker stopped counting, he/she yelled, "Come out, come out, wherever you are," and began looking for the hiders. The seeker might look behind a garbage can, under steps, behind a bush, just anywhere someone might be able to hide. While the seeker was looking, the hiders would try to make it back to the base before being tagged. If the seeker found and tagged the hider before he/she made it back to base, the hider would be captured by the seeker. This was such a fun game. We would just laugh, laugh, and laugh. Well, we would also argue a little if we thought the seeker or hider was cheating. Sometimes a player would hide so well that the seeker couldn't find him/her. Eventually, the seeker would have to give up and request the player come out of the hiding spot; then the game would start all over again.

As a child, I would also hide different things that I would seek out later. I would hide candy and other stuff or maybe my true feelings about a certain matter. I would also hide some valuable information about something I did or said. Sometimes, I would hide stuff and forget about it. I remember I hid some food in my pocket and forgot about it. I think my Mom found it because an odor was coming out of the closet. There are also some things that I hid that no one knows about except God because there is nothing I or anyone can hide from Him.

Most of us are aware that there is nothing that we can hide from God. However, we still find ourselves trying to hide stuff. Adam and Eve hid

237

after they had bitten the fruit that God had commanded them not to eat (Gen. 3). Jonah tried to hide from God because he no longer wanted to do what God had requested of him (Jonah 1-2). David tried to hide his adulterous relationship with Bathsheba by having her husband killed (2 Sam. 11-12). Adam, Eve, Jonah and David's sins were not hidden from God. God would reveal their sin to them. Out of God's love and justice, He spoke to each of them about their sin. Each of them humbled themselves and repented.

God would have us not to hide our sin from Him but to bring it to His throne of grace and mercy. At any point in time, Adam, Eve, Jonah, and David could have brought their issue before the Lord. Eve could have rebuked the serpent and called on the help of the Lord. Adam could have called on God before he ate of the forbidden fruit. Jonah could have presented his anger to the Lord rather than trying to run and hide. Upon seeing Bathsheba and desiring her, David could have talked to God about His desire and asked Him to have mercy and show him how to turn from the desire to have Bathsheba, the wife of Uriah.

I know our flesh and defenses can keep us from doing the right thing; however, doing the right thing is always available and so is God. At any point in our situation, we can reveal our sin to God, repent, and move forward in His mercy and grace. God knows what's going on. God knows everything about us, and He still loves us.

Don't try to play Hide and Go Seek with God. It is impossible to hide your sin from the "Master Seeker" (Ps. 139). It is His will that we put our sin before Him. Just come before Him with a repentant heart. He is a just and loving God and will forgive you of your sin (1 Jn. 1:9). He will also walk with

> *God knows everything about us, and He still loves us.*

you as you face the consequences of your sin. God will make a way out. His Word says, "And we know that all things work together for good to them that love God, to them who are the called according to His purpose" (Rom. 8:28). Do you trust and love God? If so, know that all things in your life will work out according to His divine purpose.

Come out, come out wherever you are. You will be happy God tagged you and said, "You're it. You are my child, and I love you.

Faith Affirmation: *God knows everything about me, and He still loves me.*

Prayer: Lord, I thank You for this day (Ps. 118:24). You are great and mighty, and Your mercy endures forever (Ps. 136:1). Lord, it is my desire to show myself to You. I want You to "Search me, O God, and know my heart: try me, and know my thoughts: and see if there be any wicked way in me, and lead me in the way everlasting" (Ps. 139:23-24). I thank You for tagging me.

Dear God Letter: Talk to God about your day. **Come out, Come out, wherever you are** and talk to God about it.

Dear God,

YOUR BEFORE

Brethren, I count not myself to have apprehended: but this one thing I do, forgetting those things which are behind, and reaching forth unto those things which are before, I press toward the mark for the prize of the high calling of God in Christ Jesus (Phil. 3:13-14).

The Word that stands out in this scripture is *before*. Your *before* is what has not been obtained but is thus far your hope; "For we are saved by hope: but hope that is seen is not hope: for what a man seeth, why does he yet hope for? But if we hope for what we see not, then do we with patience wait for it" (Rom. 8:24-25). The Word is clear: "Now faith is the substance of things hoped for, the evidence of things not seen" (Heb. 11:1). If you can't see by faith that you are pressing to *your before*, then the Word is not going to benefit you. Your before is the mountain you need to be removed. Many people pray, God remove this mountain and expect that the mountain will be removed within hours or days. However, when your faith is telling you that the mountain is removed, you will not be moved by what you hear, see, or feel; *your before* is prepared to arrive in God's perfect time.

> *Your before is prepared to arrive in God's perfect time.*

Your before is your impossibility but God's possibility! Your before could be using your gifts and talents to build up God's kingdom; *your before* could be getting a new job; starting a new business; beginning a new ministry; *having* boldness to tell others about the resurrected Christ; *laying hands on someone in the name of Jesus and they are* healed; restoring your marriage; *asking God for* forgiveness; *receiving* substance abuse freedom; *claiming* financial stability; possessing the land; replacing seating in your church; or whatever you are pressing to get to every day. Your before can be simple to some and complex to others. The Word is clear, "I will go before thee, and make the crooked places straight" (Isa. 45:2), and thus, you will receive *your before*.

As I was sitting in traffic one day, God clearly said to me, "Your before is getting home and you are pressing to get there. You stop, you go, you get cut off, you call My Son's name, you almost hit another car, you call My Son's name, you pray, you worship, and you listen to praise music. Whatever you need to do to get home you continue to do it until you get there. Similarly, as we press to get home (heaven) to be with our Father, we must also do all that God has called us to do to get there; this is *our before*.

No one can determine if you are pressing to get to *your before* but you and Jesus. God knows your heart and your plans. He also knows what He has planned for your life (Jer. 29:11). Continue to press for *your before* and "for the prize of the high calling of God in Christ Jesus" (Phil. 3:14). Yes, you will have many unsettling moments, but you will also have many joyous moments. No matter the moment or situation, you must hold on to the One, who says, "I am with you always, even unto the end of the world." (Matt. 28:20).

Faith Affirmation: *I am reaching for those things which are before me in Jesus' name.*

Prayer: Lord, I thank You for this day (Ps. 118:24). I will "praise [Your] great and [awesome] name; for it is holy" (Ps. 99:3). "For as the heaven is high above the earth, so great is [Your] mercy toward [me]" (Ps. 103:11). I press toward my *before*. I press "toward the mark for the prize of the high calling of God in Jesus Christ" (Phil. 3:14). No matter the situation, I will hold on to You. You have great plans for my life and will lead me into Your perfect way.

Dear God Letter: Talk to God about your day. Remember to reach for **your before** and to press daily to fulfill your calling in the name of Jesus.

Dear God,

Date:
Day #:

GREAT!

*Great is the LORD, and greatly to be praised; and His greatness
is unsearchable (Ps. 145:3).*

Read the scriptures below. Then read them again and fill in the word
"great" with one of the synonyms (immeasurable, infinite, etc.). For
example, Great is the Lord, and greatly to be praised, and His greatness
is unsearchable. Then read, Immeasurable is the Lord, and greatly to be
praised. Allow God's greatness to bless your heart and spirit.

Great – immeasurable, infinite, incalculable, endless, beyond measure,
eternal, timeless, ceaseless, never-ending, faithful, everlasting, excellent,
absolute, perfect, faultless, . . .

♥

"**Great** is [my] Lord, and of great power: His understanding is infinite"
(Ps. 147:5).

♥

"For as the heaven is high above the earth, so **great** is His mercy toward
them that fear Him" (Ps. 103:11).

♥

"For the LORD is **great**, and greatly to be praised: He is to be feared
above all gods" (Ps. 96:4).

♥

"For thy mercy is **great** unto the heavens, and thy truth unto the clouds"
(Ps. 57:10).

♥

"Oh how **great** is thy goodness, which thou hast laid up for them that fear
thee . . ." (Ps. 31:19).

245

♥

"O LORD, how **great** are thy works! And thy thoughts are very deep"
(Ps. 92:5).

♥

"For the LORD is a **great** God, and a great King above all gods"
(Ps. 95:3).

♥

"[I will] praise thy **great** and [awesome] name; for it is holy" (Ps. 99:3).

♥

"For I know that the LORD is **great**, and that [my] LORD is above all
gods. Whatsoever the LORD pleased, that did He in heaven, and in earth,
in the seas, and all deep places" (Ps. 135:5-6).

We cannot comprehend the greatness of our Lord. "His greatness is
unsearchable" (Ps. 145:3). His greatness goes beyond what we have read or
been told about Him. Our Lord is **great** and "**great** is [His] mercy toward
[us]" (Ps. 86:13). He is **great** no matter how we feel or what we believe.
It is an undeniable fact that God is **great** —"full of compassion, and gracious, long suffering, and plenteous in mercy and truth" (Ps. 86:15). What
a mighty and **great** God we serve.

Faith Affirmation: *The Lord is **great**, and I will forever praise His name.*

Prayer: Lord, I thank You for another day to acknowledge Your greatness
(Ps. 118:24). "Every day will I bless thee; and I will praise thy name forever and ever" (Ps. 145:2). "For You are "**great** and greatly to be praised"
(Ps. 96:4). I will "praise thy **great** and [awesome] name; for it is holy" (Ps.
99:3). "Even from everlasting to everlasting, thou art God" (Ps. 90:2) and
worthy to be praised.

Dear God Letter: Talk to God about your day. **God is great!**

Dear God,

VICTORY BEYOND BONDAGE

And Paul dwelt two whole years in his own hired house (confinement in Rome). . .Preaching the kingdom of God, and teaching those things which concern the Lord Jesus Christ, with all confidence, no man forbidding him (Acts 28:30-31).

S aul was a persecutor of those who confessed the gospel of Jesus Christ. He witnessed and consented to the murder of Stephen, a disciple of Jesus Christ (Acts 7:54-60; 8:1). He also made havoc of the church, entering into the homes of Christians to persecute and put them in prison (Acts 8:3). The persecution of the believers caused many of them to flee to different regions for fear of their lives. God used their escape as an opportunity for them to get reestablished in new regions and spread the gospel of Jesus Christ (Acts 8:4).

As Saul continued to seek out those who confessed the name of Jesus Christ to imprison or kill them, the Lord met him on the road to Damascus. The Lord

> "shined round about him a light from heaven: And [Saul] fell to the earth, and heard a voice saying unto him, Saul, Saul why persecutest thou me? And he said, Who art thou, Lord? And the Lord said, I am Jesus whom thou persecutest. . . And he trembling and astonished said, Lord, what wilt thou have me to do?" (Acts 9:1-6).

It was this encounter with the Lord that led to Saul's conversion and love for Christ. In that moment, Saul made a commitment to serve the Lord no matter the cost. As a servant of the Lord, he went before the high priests and shared the gospel of Jesus Christ, and he was rejected and imprisoned. He and other missionaries set up churches in Europe. He spoke in Jewish synagogues where he preached salvation for Jews and gentiles. He was expelled from cities and severely beaten; yet, he continued to preach the Word of God with great zeal and passion.

At one point in his ministry, Saul, now known as Paul, was imprisoned in Rome for two years. While in detention, Paul preached the kingdom of God, and taught the people concerning the Lord Jesus Christ, with all confidence to all who would hear (Acts 28:30-31). In fact, he wrote epistles to several churches: Philippians, Ephesians, Colossians, and Philemon, each letter dealt with the issues they were facing and reminded them of the importance of living godly lives and preaching the gospel of Jesus Christ. No matter his circumstance, Paul was not ashamed of the gospel of Christ. He knew that the gospel was "the power of God unto salvation to every one that believeth; to the Jew first, and also to the Greek" (Rom. 1:16).

Paul did not allow his circumstances to overshadow His calling to preach, teach, write, and establish God's Word. He knew that He could lose his life, but it was imperative that He do the will of God. He was pressing "toward the mark for the prize of the high calling of God in Christ Jesus" (Phil. 3:14), the reward that He would receive from God when he reached heaven. He could only be victorious in what he did for Christ.

We have all experienced, may be experiencing or will experience extremely difficult and challenging times in our lives. Have you come to a place where you can say, Lord, I have no control over my situation; I place it in Your hands. Whatever my situation, I will praise Your Holy name. I will tell others about You. I will speak of Your many blessings. I will share my testimony. I will remain diligent in my quest to draw closer to You. I am confident of this very thing that I will do the will of God, and one day I will meet my Father and hear Him say, "Well done my good and faithful servant" (Matt. 25:21).

Take the time to write a letter of victory even if your life circumstances don't appear to be victorious when looking through the eyes of the flesh. However, in the Spirit, you are always victorious through Christ Jesus.

Faith Affirmation: *I am victorious in the name of Jesus Christ.*

Prayer: Father, I thank You for another day to live in Your liberty (Gal. 5:1). I will rejoice and be glad (Ps. 118:24). I will speak of Your many blessings (Ps. 68:19). I will remain committed to sharing Your Word and the Good News of Jesus Christ with others. I will remain diligent in my quest to draw closer to You. Lord, I am confident of this very thing that I will do Your will, and one day I will meet You and hear You say, "Well done my good and faithful servant" (Matt. 25:21).

Dear God Letter: Talk to God about your day. Remember challenges in your day or life should not prevent you from speaking and teaching the message of our Lord Jesus Christ. You have **victory beyond your bondage** in the name of Jesus.

Dear God,

Date:

Day #:

A NEEDLE IN A HAYSTACK

But as it is written, Eye hath not seen, nor ear heard, neither have entered into the heart of man, the things which God hath prepared for them that love Him (1 Cor. 2:9).

Sometimes we find ourselves searching for a missing something in our lives. You wonder why certain situations have happened to you. You feel as if you weren't loved, cared for, or protected. You feel as if something is missing in your life. You find yourself looking for a new you, a loved one, or someone who has done something inappropriate to you or someone you love. This search for what is missing consumes a big piece of your life and you want and need an answer. Resolving the situation seems to be like looking for a *needle in a haystack*; yet, you keep searching and holding on to your hope in the Lord. God sees all things, knows all things and most definitely knows the location of your missing something.

A friend of mine had been seeking the Lord regarding a missing something in her life. She was adopted at a young age and wanted God to help her find her parents, specifically her mother. For as long as she can remember, she put her prayer request before the Lord and sought assistance from Him to locate her parents. She also experienced personal turmoil as she searched for her parents and the meaning of her life. She would hear about others finding their family and wonder why God had not allowed her to find her family. What had she done to deserve this? God heard the cries of His child and continued to hold her in his loving arms and minister to her heart. As the years went by, she became less focused on finding her parents and more focused on "discovering herself." God walked and talked with her every step of the way. He provided her with new insights and helped her understand that she was a child of the Most High God (Ps. 97:9). He had a divine purpose for her life and desired that she draw closer to Him. She continued to seek the Lord and allowed Him to be the light of her life. It wasn't always easy, but God made it possible.

253

In her mid-forties, God revealed what seemed to be her *needle in a hay-stack*. He revealed the location of her mother and her entire family. Praise God! Praise God! He gave her abundantly above all that she could ask or think (Eph. 3:20). And guess what; she has brothers, sisters, aunts, uncles, nephews, nieces, cousins and a healthy beautiful gray haired grandma. Her family has embraced her with open arms and overflowing love. Oh, God's love and goodness are immeasurable.

God will reveal all things and all mysteries in His time. Rejoice, knowing that there is nothing too hard for God (Jer. 32:27). He does hear the prayers of His children and will answer in His time, which is the perfect time for you.

Faith Affirmation: *God will reveal all things pertaining to me in His perfect time.*

Prayer: Lord, I thank You for another day to rejoice and be glad (Ps. 118:24). I will "bless thee Lord, O my soul: and all that is within me, bless Your holy name" (Ps. 103:1). You are the Most High God (Ps. 97:9) and know what is best for me. I sometimes struggle as I wait for You. I am reminded that if I wait on You, You will renew my strength (Isa. 40:31) and take me to a place higher than I can imagine, and that place is with You.

Dear God Letter: Talk to God about your day. God knows all things. Only He can reveal your **needle in a haystack**.

Dear God,

Date:
Day #:

A SWEET EPIPHANY

*And the angel said . . . For unto you is born this day in the city of David
a Savior, which is Christ the Lord. And this shall be a sign unto you; Ye
shall find the babe wrapped in swaddling clothes, lying in a manger.
And suddenly there was with the angel a multitude of the heavenly host
praising God, and saying, Glory to God in the highest, and on earth
peace, good will toward men (Lk. 2:10-14).*

One early morning in November 2006, I was praying to God asking
Him to help me get through the day. I prayed to God and thanked
Him for showing me His favor. I made my regular stop at the coffee shop,
which became a sweet epiphany and a life changing moment.

I walked into the coffee shop that was full of red and white snowflakes
and plenty of holiday decorations. In that moment, God reminded me that
the celebration of the birth of His Son had
begun. He filled my heart with peace and joy.
My heart and soul were overwhelmed by the
presence of the Lord. I quietly began to sing
"Oh, come let us adore Him, Oh, come let us
adore Him. Oh, come let us adore Him, Christ
the Lord." This November epiphany felt so
comforting and sweet.

*Oh, come let us
adore Him!*

I shared my story with others and reminded them to rejoice in the birth
of Christ and His return. I encouraged them not to complain about the
Christmas media frenzy that begins in October, but to rejoice at the coming
of Jesus Christ, the Messiah (Jn. 4:25, 26), the Prince of Peace (Isa. 9:6),
the Door to everlasting life (Jn. 10:9). What people have used as a way to
increase their profit, God has used to remind the world of His unconditional
love and sacrifice (Jn. 3:16).

As the year wore on, I continued to acknowledge Jesus Christ and to do
His will. Yet again, in the fall of the following year, God reminded me of

the birth of His son, Jesus Christ. While walking to my office on an overcast October morning, I looked up at a large pine tree and saw that the needles in the center of the tree had turned auburn, while the outer pine needles remained green. Then a vibrant gold light illuminated from the center of the tree; the tree appeared to be glowing. It reminded me of the burning bush and the presence of God in the story of Moses (Ex. 3:2). I paused, and in that moment I felt the sweet presence of God. He brought to my remembrance the birth of His Son Jesus Christ and all of His glory and majesty.

God reminded me that it was time to celebrate the birth of His Son. It was time to share with others the coming of the Lord. Once again, the voice of the Lord humbled me and brought forth His praise. I began to sing "Oh, come let us adore Him. Oh, come let us adore Him. Oh, come let us adore Him, Christ the Lord." I could feel God's presence. I could feel Him walking and talking with me. Most of all, I could feel His love. He reminded me ever so softly and sweetly of His love; another sweet, sweet epiphany. I began to remind others of the coming of the Lord. I reminded them of our charge to love one another as Christ loved us (Jn. 15:12) and to spread the Good News of Jesus Christ (Mk. 16:15). I reminded them to praise the Lord, for "great is the Lord and greatly to be praised; and His greatness is unsearchable" (Ps. 145:3). I also reminded them that God loves them. Oh, how He loves them.

Take the time no matter what the season to read about the birth of Christ, His works and return for His children. Take the time to share God's love and tell others about the birth of Christ, in and out of the holiday season. Praise His Holy name. Oh, come into His presence today. Sing unto the Lord, "Glory to God in the highest, Glory to God in the highest" (Lk. 2:13-14). "Oh, come let us adore Him. Oh, come let us adore Him. Oh, come let us adore Him, Christ the Lord. For He alone is worthy!"

Faith Affirmation: *Glory to God in the highest.*

Prayer: Lord, I thank You for this day (Ps. 118:24). I will forever love You and praise Your holy name (Ps. 99:3). I will take the time to tell others about the birth of Christ, in and out of the holiday season. Lord, I come in Your presence with a heart of praise singing "Glory, Glory, Glory to God in the highest, Glory to God in the highest" (Lk. 2:13-14).

Dear God Letter: Talk to God about your day. Remember, God's **sweet epiphany** will bless you and draw you closer to Him.

Dear God,

AS A ROARING LION

*Be sober, be vigilant; because your adversary the devil, as a roaring lion,
walketh about, seeking whom he may devour (1 Pet. 5:8).*

Satan comes as a roaring lion seeking whom he may devour. Keywords *roaring* (noisy, loud) lion *seeking* (looking for) whom he *may* (possibly can) *devour* (eat greedily, consume dispose of). Satan does not know for sure who he will devour (eat up or destroy). Our behavior will dictate if he may consume us. Satan comes roaring. Often if you hear a roar or a loud noise you stop in your tracks and try to locate where the roar is coming from, its proximity, and who or what (animal, object) is making the noise. So, if Satan comes as a roaring lion don't panic, you already know who is roaring. Stop in the name of Jesus and determine his location – where has he reared his ugly head? Is he roaring at your dreams and ambitions? Is he roaring at your discontentment? Is he roaring at your concerns about providing for your family? Is he roaring at your marital struggles? Is he roaring at your singleness? Is he roaring at your children? Is he roaring at your expectations? Is he roaring at your hurt and pain? Is he roaring at your health? Is he roaring at your self-confidence? Is he roaring at your faith? Is he roaring at your joy?

Is Satan roaring in your life? Well, if you're out of control, Satan is roaring. If you're not using your gifts to make a difference for others, then Satan's roaring. If you can't get your thoughts under control, then Satan is roaring. If you doubt what God clearly told you to do, then Satan is roaring. If you have lost your praise, then Satan is roaring. If you can't encourage yourself, then Satan is roaring. If you have walked out of your relationship (marriage, friendship) without God's authorization, then Satan is roaring. If you can't admit when you're wrong, then Satan is roaring. If you can't forgive others, then Satan is roaring. If you can't forgive yourself, then Satan is roaring. If you can't see your limitations or shortcomings, then Satan is roaring. If you continue to beat up on yourself, then Satan is roaring. If you've stopped dreaming, then Satan is roaring. If you don't share the Good News of Jesus Christ, then Satan is roaring. He's roaring in hopes that you will continue to stay in your condition so that he can consume you.

Satan has roared at my expectations of being a strong woman of God. When I don't feel like I've met that expectation, I can hear those thoughts that tell me I'm a disappointment to my Father. As I entertain those thoughts, Satan begins to bring in a flood of negative thoughts and images. But, when I catch on to Satan's lies, I rebuke him in the name of Jesus and cast him down under my feet in the name of Jesus. I speak forth those things that I know about being God's child. I am fearfully and wonderfully made (Ps. 139:14). I

Is Satan roaring in your life?

am the apple of God's eye (Ps. 17:8). Surely, if His eye is on the sparrow, I know He watches over me (Matt. 10:29-31). I am made in His image and likeness (Gen. 1:26); therefore I will bear His fruit (Gal. 5:22). He is a God who forgives (1 Jn. 1:9). My shortcomings are God's opportunities to build my character and help me to become more like Him. I will rejoice in the Lord (Phil. 4:4). I will encourage myself in the name of Jesus. God loves me and is with "[me] always unto the end of the world" (Matt. 28:20). I am victorious!

To cease Satan's roaring you must (1) Know that God is God (Isa. 45:5-6). (2) Submit to God (Jas. 4:7). (3) Check your shield of faith and trust God (Eph. 6:16; Prov. 3:5). (4) Pull out the sword of the Spirit, which is the Word of God (Eph. 6:17). (5) Resist Satan (Jas. 4:7). (6) Call out those things that are honest, right, just and empowering (Phil. 4:8). (7) Release God's powerful Word which is sharper than any twoedged sword (Heb. 4:12) cutting through your condition and shutting down Satan.

Come to God's throne of grace that you may obtain mercy and embrace His love (Heb. 4:16). God will speak to you and once again affirm that He loves you. He is your Father and is always with you –just call out His name – Jesus, Jesus, Jesus and at the mention of His name "every knee shall bow, of things in heaven, and things in earth, and things under the earth; and that every tongue should confess that Jesus Christ is Lord, to the glory of God the Father" (Phil. 2:10-11).

Faith Affirmation: *I have the victory in the name of Jesus.*

Prayer: Lord, I am grateful that You called this day into existence for me (Ps. 118:24).You are "my rock and my fortress; therefore for thy name's sake lead me, and guide me" (Ps. 31:3). Lord, Satan comes as a roaring lion seeking to devour me (1 Pet. 5:8). You have "come that [I] might have life, and that [I] might have it more abundantly" (Jn. 10:10). I will resist Satan in the name of Jesus, and he shall flee from me (Jas. 4:7). I have the victory!

Dear God Letter: Talk to God about your day. Satan comes as **a roaring lion** seeking to devour you. Fear not; God comes with strength, power, and life.

Dear God,

Date:
Day #:

BOW DOWN AND WORSHIP GOD

O come, let us worship and bow down: let us kneel before the LORD our maker. For He is our God; and we are the people of His pasture, and the sheep of his hand. . . (Ps. 95:6-7).

Lord, You are an awesome God. I praise Your name. **I worship and adore You.** You alone are worthy to be praised. You alone are worthy. I bow down before You and worship You. **I bless Your holy name.** I acknowledge Your love for me and Your people. You alone are worthy of all the glory, praise and worship. **I bless Your name and praise You.** I live, breathe, and have my being because of You (Acts 17:28). I was created by You and am fearfully and wonderfully made (Ps. 139:14). You are an awesome Father. There is none like You (Isa. 43:10-11). There is no one or thing worthy of Your praise. **I praise Your holy name.** You sent Your Son, Jesus, to bless Your people and bring us into a right relationship with You. Jesus hung on the cross and died for our sins that we might be reconciled to You, God the Father, the creator of the heavens and earth and all that exist (Ps. 24:1). You offered me the gift of salvation (Eph. 2:8-9). You filled me with You, the Holy Spirit (1 Cor. 3:16), and renewed my soul. Lord, I have so much to be thankful for. **I worship and adore You.** You have brought me through trials and tribulations. You have brought me a mighty long way. You created me in Your image and likeness (Gen. 1:26). You are love. Your love is everlasting to everlasting (1 Jn. 4:8-10). Your peace surpasses all understanding (Phil. 4:7). Your joy is an unspeakable joy (1 Pet. 1:6-9). Your correction is done in love and for my benefit (Prov. 3:12). **I bow down and worship You.** Your presence is breathtaking.

Lord, I heard You today in the laughter of the children. I felt You today in the smiles of people. I saw You in the beautiful colored leaves on the trees. I felt You as the rain sprinkled my brow. I smelled Your sweet fragrance as I inhaled the fresh air. You softly touched me as I read Your Word. I tasted You as I read the Bread of life. I embraced You as You called, "Come unto me, all ye that labor and are heavy laden, and I will give you rest" (Matt. 11:28). I fell asleep with You and heard You whisper, "I love you."

Lord, my soul cries out thank You for saving and blessing me. My soul cries out with words of praise and worship. My soul cries out Lord, I love You.

Will you worship with me today? Will you take the time to praise His holy name? Stop right now and praise His name. Open your heart and feel His presence. Open your heart and praise His name. Hail, Hail, King Jesus! Open your heart and receive His love. **Open your heart and bow down in your spirit and worship GOD in spirit and in truth** (Jn. 4:24). He is God, and "there is no God beside Him. . ." (Isa. 45:5-7).

Faith Affirmation: *I will bow down and worship the Lord.*

Prayer: Lord, I thank You for another day to bow down and worship You (Ps. 118:24). I will bless You always and forever (Ps. 115:18). You are perfect in all Your ways (Ps. 18:30). You are a great and awesome God (Ps. 99:3). I worship and adore You. I bow down before You and worship You (Ps. 95:6-7). I acknowledge Your love for me and Your people. You alone are worthy of all the glory, praise, and worship.

Dear God Letter: Talk to God about your day. Remember to **bow down and worship God**. He is your creator who offers you eternal life.

Dear God,

Date:

Day #:

SOMEONE'S GOT TO DO IT

Ye have not chosen me, but I have chosen you, and ordained you, that ye should go and bring forth fruit. . . (Jn. 15:16).

A woman was constantly talking on the telephone with her friends and family. She always kept up with the latest news about what was going on with different folks and was more than willing to share the information with others. She was also immensely helpful and would do anything for family and friends. She was asked why she spent so much time keeping up with the gossip – I mean the latest news. She replied "Someone's got to do it. Someone's got to help others and make sure they know what's going on."

A man of prominence and stature in the church and community spent a good portion of his day criticizing people. At church, he would criticize the church programs and members who agreed to help make a difference. At work, he criticized the work of his colleagues and staff. At home, he criticized his wife and children. Oh yeah, he called it constructive feedback. When asked why he spent so much time providing feedback, he replied, "Someone's got to do it. Someone's got to help people get it right."

An older woman went outside each morning and kept an eye out on the school children. She always reminded them to have a good day and to do their best. She often gave them extra snacks for their lunch just in case some of them didn't have a lunch or enough to eat. She also went to the hospital and visited the sick. She cooked great meals for those shut-in due to illness. She made it her business to share a kind word. She softly yet boldly showed the love of God and told people about her Savior. Someone asked her, why did she always have a kind and encouraging word? Why did she get up and watch the school children none of whom were her children? Where did she find the time and strength to do so much? The woman replied, "I have been

Someone's got to do it, and God chose you.

called to be a servant of God. I do what is required of me by God. If not me, then who? Someone's got to do it, and God chose me."

We can choose to do those things that tear people down or those things that edify and build up people and the kingdom of God. As Christians, we have been chosen by God to love one another (Jn. 15:12), to bear the fruit of the Spirit (Gal. 5:22-23), to share His love, and to tell others about the Good News of Jesus Christ (Mk. 16:15). If not you, then who? Someone's got to do it, and God chose you.

Faith Affirmation: *I have been chosen by God to share His love.*

Prayer: Lord, this is the day that You made for me (Ps. 118:24). I will bless You with all that is within me (Ps. 103:1) from this day forward and forever. You are the creator of the heavens and earth and all that is within it (Ps. 24:1). Before You formed me in my mother's womb, You called and purposed me (Jer. 1:5). Lord, it is You who works in me to do Your will and good pleasure (Phil. 2:13). "I press toward the mark for the prize of the high calling of God in Christ Jesus" (Phil. 3:14). If not me, then who?

Dear God Letter: Talk to God about your day. Remember every day holds an opportunity for you to share the love of Jesus Christ. **Someone's got to do it, and God chose you.**

Dear God,

Date:
Day #:

CAREER CHOICE

But now hath God set the members every one of them in the body, as it hath pleased Him (1 Cor. 12:18).

As an adolescent, my daughter began talking more and more about career choices. You know, what she wanted to be when she grew up. She was wondering if she would become a scientist, chef, or representative fighting against injustices. One day my daughter told me she was getting stressed about choosing a career. I reminded her that she was young and had plenty of time to make a career decision. Right now, she could continue to explore and dream. As I thought about my daughter's conversation with me and my own career exploration, I realized that at her age, I had only focused on a professional career, not my Christian career or calling. I don't recall thinking about what career God called me to fulfill in the kingdom.

When I got older and accepted Christ into my life, the Lord spoke to me and told me that he had called me to be a teacher and speaker in the kingdom, and most recently a writer administering my gifts in love. He has called all of His children to kingdom careers in "one body, and one Spirit, even as ye are called in one hope of your calling; one Lord, one faith, one baptism, one God and Father of all, who is above all, and through all, and in you all" (Eph. 4:4-6).

What career has God called for you in the kingdom? What gifts have God placed within you? (1 Cor. 12:4). Has He called you to be an encourager, teacher, preacher, usher, writer, missionary, caretaker, counselor, evangelist, vocalist, dancer, and so on? If you ask, God will give you insight into your career in the kingdom. He has already called you and prepared you for it. You just need to step into your career and follow His guidance and direction. Remember, what God has called He has also anointed and will complete it (1 Thess. 5:24; Phil. 1:6).

Faith Affirmation: *I will become what God called me to be.*

Prayer: Lord, I thank You for another opportunity to rejoice and be glad today (Ps. 118:24). "How excellent is [Your] name in all the earth!" (Ps. 8:1). Lord, I will stir up my God-given gifts and use them to build up the kingdom and fulfill my purpose (2 Tim. 1:6). You are faithful and have called me to make a difference (1 Thess. 5:24), and I will do so in Your name.

Dear God Letter: Talk to God about your day. Remember **your career in the kingdom** has been called by God.

Dear God,

NAKED I CAME

♡♡

And [Job] said, Naked came I out of my mother's womb, and naked shall
I return thither. . . (Job 1:21).

Life tosses so many different circumstances our way, with each requiring that we seek God for help. It is through these circumstances that our character is built, our faith is strengthened and our lives are transformed. As we seek God, we have the opportunity to learn more about Him, draw closer to Him and become more like Christ.

Life is full of the good and bad and the ups and downs. If you don't remember that life comes with adversities that shape your character and spiritual identity, you will get frustrated and quite disappointed. You may also become fearful, discouraged, and bitter. You will find yourself making decisions out of your frustration, disappointment, and fear, leaving you to do some crazy stuff.

I recall a situation where I forgot that God was building my character. By the time it had dawned on me, I was naked. I had been struggling with issues on my job. I couldn't seem to talk about anything but my job. My competence felt like it was being questioned and challenged. Oh, this was major. I had put a lot of time in my education to ensure that I was competent. Well, something happened at work that led me to believe that I had possibly made a "huge" error that would probably require a verbal or written disciplinary action.

I couldn't think about anything but this situation. I ran the scenario over and over in my head. It's no way that I would have made that mistake. I became anxious and was having difficulty focusing. While parking my car in the airport garage, I stopped and decided to get my luggage out before I completed my parking. I got out of my car and lifted up my hatchback so that I could get my luggage out. I got my luggage out. I jumped back into my car and forgot to let down my hatchback, which resulted in me running my hatchback into the cement post and denting my hatchback. This really set me off. My thoughts got quite irrational, and I became very agitated.

Once I arrived at my destination, I checked in my hotel room. I wasn't thinking clearly at all. While in my room that night, the Lord interrupted my irrational thoughts. He reminded me to come to His throne. I got out of my bed and got naked before the Lord. I paced up and down my room praising the Lord. I cried out frantically unto the Lord, "Naked, I was. Naked, I thought. Naked, I came. Naked, I am" – and I was literally naked. Oh, you can start laughing now. I'm laughing as I'm writing this.

> *Naked I came to God's throne.*

I was desperate for an answer. I think I shouted, "Lord, Oh Lord, where art thou." I think I also mixed in a little rap. "A hip hop to the hippity hop please don't stop, Lord; I need to hear from You." I'm sure by this time the Lord was even cracking up. I pulled out some other songs: "Have you seen Him tell me have you seen Him. Lord, You are my hero. You're everything I hoped for and long to be. Great are Your mercies toward me; Your lovingkindness toward me. Your tender mercies I see day after day." I think I wrapped it up with "I need thee; oh, I need thee; every hour I need thee. I love You. I love You. I love You, Lord, today because You cared for me in such a special way." Alright, I did adlib a little, but you get the point. I was desperately seeking a word from God.

The Lord heard my heartfelt cry and wrapped His loving arms around me. He comforted me and spoke to my heart. He reminded me to trust Him and that no harm would come to me. He reminded me that people can do nothing unto me (Ps. 118:6). He asked me if I would trust Him. Would I praise Him no matter the circumstance? I replied, "Yes, Lord." I surrendered my will and adversity to God. I fell asleep wrapped in God's love. When I awakened, He opened my mind and allowed me to see that I had not made a mistake and that it would be brought to light upon my return to work.

That day I sang new songs. "What a friend I have in Jesus. What a privilege to carry everything to God in prayer." "I surrender all. All to thee my blessed Savior, I surrender all." "He is my rock, my sword, my shield" and in Him will I trust. "I love You. I love You. I love You Lord today because You cared for me in such a special way." He alone is God and worthy to be praised!

Faith Affirmation: *Lord, I stand naked before You seeking Your blessings.*

Prayer: Lord, it is through Your grace and mercy that You allowed me to have another day to rejoice and be glad (Ps. 118:24).You are a wonderful and awesome God (Ps. 145:3). You have considered my trouble and delivered me (Ps. 121). I will not fear but trust You (Ps. 62:8). "You hath not given [me] the spirit of fear; but of power, and of love, and of a sound mind" (2 Tim. 1:7). Lord, I stand naked before You seeking a word from You.

Dear God Letter: Talk to God about your day. Remember in **your naked moments** to trust God and praise Him for being your comforter.

Dear God,

A STRANGE THING HAPPENED ON THE WAY TO A BLESSING

And, behold, there cometh one of the rulers of the synagogue, Jairus by name; and when he saw [Jesus], he fell at His feet, And besought Him greatly saying, My little daughter lieth at the point of death: I pray thee, come and lay thy hands on her, that she may be healed; and she shall live (Mk. 5:22-23).

Jesus had traveled with his twelve disciples throughout the cities and villages teaching and proclaiming the kingdom of God (Lk. 8:1). He also cast out the many demons that possessed a man (Lk. 8:28-40). Upon completing His work, Jesus and the disciples crossed a lake where a multitude of people awaited them. The people were waiting for the man who had the power to heal, work miracles, and cast out demons. They were waiting for Jesus, the Messiah.

When Jesus arrived at His destination, Jairus, a ruler of the synagogue, had made it to the front of the awaiting crowd. He had an urgent matter to put before Jesus. Jairus, a man of power and stature, fell at the feet of Jesus and besought Him saying, "My little daughter lieth at the point of death: I pray thee come and lay thy hands on her, that she may be healed; and she shall live" (Mk. 5:22-23). Jesus responded to his request and proceeded to go with Jairus to heal his daughter. However, this was a difficult task because the multitude of people thronged Him; they pressed up against Him (Mk. 5:24). They, too, were in need of a blessing from Jesus. Can't you hear Jairus pleading with the people "Move out of our way; my daughter is dying and we don't have much time? Please back up. We don't have much time." Yet, amongst all the noise and commotion, the people continued to throng Jesus.

There was a certain woman, who was also pressing in the crowd in hopes of being healed by Jesus. This woman had an issue of blood for 12 years that could not be cured by the physicians or home remedies (Mk. 5:25-26). She so desperately needed to be healed. She said, "If I may touch but His clothes, I shall be whole" (Mk. 5:28). She pressed with the crowd and somehow a space opened up, and she reached down with her heartfelt faith and touched the hem of Jesus' garment and immediately she was healed (Mk. 5:29). Jesus turned about, which placed Him in a different direction and said, "Who touched my clothes?" (Mk. 5:30).

Oh my goodness, Jesus had paused in the middle of Jairus' crisis. He had paused to ask, who touched Him (Mk. 5:31). There was a multitude of people; anyone could have touched Him. Didn't he know Jairus' daughter was dying? Hadn't he promised to come to Jairus' house and heal his daughter? Jairus had to wonder what was going on. He needed Jesus to hurry. How could Jesus pause while his daughter lay dying? Jairus needed Jesus to stay focused and get to his house and heal his daughter.

While the prophets and Jairus are wondering what's going on, the woman who had touched Jesus' garment is thinking, I'm healed. Oh, my Lord, I'm healed. With the crowd of people looking on and fear in her heart, she fell before Jesus and told Him that she had touched Him and had been healed (Mk. 5:33). Jesus said, "Daughter, thy faith hath made thee whole; go in peace, and be whole of thy plague" (Mk. 5:34). Now, this had taken time because Jesus waited for the woman to come forth, and He took the time to speak to her. It appeared that He had turned his attention from Jairus' crisis to engage the woman. Jesus was blessing her; yet, Jairus' daughter lay dying.

And while he spoke, someone from Jairus' house made it through the crowd where Jesus and Jairus stood. *The someone* said to Jairus, "Thy daughter is dead: why troublest thou the Master any further?" (Mk. 5:35). Someone had come to deliver the disappointing news to Jarius and added that since his daughter was dead, he needed to stop troubling Jesus. Not, "Jairus your daughter is dead; come immediately" or "Jairus, your daughter is dead; how sad"; but

> *Be not afraid,*
> *only believe.*

"Jairus your daughter is dead; just give up on your petition and leave the Master alone." I believe a minister once said, "There is always someone who can press through the crowd and deliver a discouraging or defeating word."

As soon as Jesus heard the words spoken to Jairus by *the someone*, He said unto Jairus, "Be not afraid, only believe" (Mk. 5:36). Basically, don't worry about what *the someone* has told you. What did I tell you? What did I promise you? I am God and cannot lie. I promised to heal your daughter, and I will heal her. It is I who has the power over life and death (Jn. 11:25-26). Don't look to the left or right, just toward me. Yes, there has been a delay, but that delay does not change my promise. You just saw the woman who had faith receive her healing. Stand on your faith, and your daughter will be healed – only believe.

I wonder how long it took for Jairus and Jesus to arrive at Jairus' home. Was it five minutes, 15 minutes, an hour or hours? It was probably the longest walk Jairus would ever take. But, it was a walk with the One who had the power to heal and to do the unimaginable.

Does it feel like God has taken a pause on His way to heal your crisis or life circumstance? Has *the someone* made it into your life, bringing words of discouragement? Are you looking around asking why is so and so being blessed by God and not me? Why did my good friend receive her blessing, but I'm still waiting? Has God forgotten about His promise that I would prosper? Has he forgotten that I need a healing? Has He forgotten that the loss of my loved one has left me sad and empty? Has He forgotten that I need an answer to my singleness? God has not forgotten you, and what appears to be a delay is really God moving in His own perfect time. A minister once stated, "A blessing delayed is not a promise denied." God's perfect time offers you an opportunity to hold on to His hope and increase your trust and faith in Him. **Be not afraid, only believe**.

Faith Affirmation: *I will not be afraid; I will only believe.*

Prayer: Lord, what a great day You have given me (Ps. 118:24). "Because thy lovingkindness is better than life, my lips shall praise thee" (Ps. 63:3). As I stand in Your presence, I will fear not "for [You] hath not given [me] the spirit of fear; but of power, and of love, and of a sound mind" (2 Tim. 1:7). I will not be afraid; I will trust in You and only believe (Mk. 5:36). I believe that You have the answer to my situation. I also believe that what You have in store for my life "shall not return unto [You] void, but it shall accomplish that which [You] please, and it shall prosper in the thing whereto [You] sent it" (Isa. 55:11). I believe that You love me. Oh, how You love me. I will stand in faith and only believe.

Dear God Letter: Talk to God about your day. Remember **a strange thing can happen on the way to your blessing**. Only Believe.

275

Dear God,

Date:

Day #:

YOUR LIFE STORY

Before the mountains were brought forth, or ever thou hadst formed the earth and the world, even from everlasting to everlasting thou art God (Ps. 90:2).

From everlasting to everlasting, He is God (Ps. 90:2). David, a man after God's own heart (Acts 13:22), and one who followed the will of God, as well as found himself on his knees repenting before the Lord, embraced God's love. David knew that God was ever present and sovereign and no matter his life circumstances, he should always seek God. For without God, he was nothing and could do nothing. David constantly sought the Lord and talked with Him. He sought the Lord with all his heart and soul. David wrote, "As the [deer] panteth after the water brooks so panteth my soul after thee, O God" (Ps. 42:1). David loved the Lord.

As a young adolescent, David was called from the sheep field by his father at the request of God's prophet, Samuel. God had ordained Samuel to anoint David as king. Neither David nor his father had any idea that David was going to be crowned king of Israel. Yet, God had written this chapter in David's life. Wow, what a day. It was this day that Samuel anointed David, and the Spirit of the Lord came upon David (1 Sam. 16:11-13), and he began his journey to take his rightful seat as the anointed king of Israel. David's life story was to have many peaks and valleys. His faith in and commitment to God was to be challenged by both external and internal forces. Even so, David always would remember that God was the author of his life story, and would turn to Him in his moments of deepest sorrow and regret.

When the army of Israel was afraid to stand up against Goliath, David stood up and killed the giant. The people praised David, and King Saul became jealous of David and sought to kill him. In an attempt to escape from King Saul's wrath, David hid in the Philistine's territory. While in this territory, the Amalekites, the enemies of Israel, kidnapped the children and wives of the men of David's armies. The men of King David's army became extremely angry and disappointed. They blamed David for putting them and their families in this state of affairs and considered stoning David. In this extremely trying situation, David made the choice to encourage himself in the Lord and sought God for direction (1 Sam. 30:1-8).

Once the king of Israel, David accomplished many great deeds, but he also sinned, which was not pleasing unto the Lord. At one point in David's kingship, he had an affair with Bathsheba, the wife of Uriah. Uriah was one of the leaders of David's army. Bathsheba conceived a child by David. In hopes of covering up his sin with Bathsheba, David had Bathsheba's husband Uriah killed on the battlefield (2 Sam. 11:14-17). David's adulterous relationship with Bathsheba and the murder of Uriah displeased the Lord (2 Sam. 11:27). David had despised the commandment of the Lord and done evil in God's sight (2 Sam. 12:9). God sent Nathan, the prophet, to rebuke David and render His judgment. After hearing God's decision, David repented, fasted and sought the Lord. He hoped God would change His judgment, but if He did not, he would continue to serve God. David loved and reverenced God (2 Sam. 12).

King David also experienced significant family conflicts and hardships. His son Amnon raped Tamar, who was Amnon's half-sister (2 Sam. 13). When King David heard of the rape, he became very angry, but he did not punish his son (2 Sam. 13:21). Two years later, David's son, Absalom, who was Tamar's full brother, avenged the assault against his sister by ordering Amnon's death (2 Sam. 13:23-29). Years later, Absalom would attempt to overthrow King David, by executing a revolt against his father. David had to flee for his life (2 Sam. 15). While on the run from Absalom, David worshiped God and sought Him for comfort and guidance (Ps. 3:1-8). As the anointed king of Israel, David knew that God was with him.

In a major battle to overthrow King David, Absalom would be killed. Upon hearing about the death of Absalom, David wept and said "Oh my son Absalom, my son, my son Absalom! Would God I had died for thee, O Absalom, my son, my son!" (2 Sam. 18:33). King David grieved and sought the Lord knowing that only God could minister to his sorrow and pain.

As David lived and breathed, he reverenced God and acknowledged that God existed in every line and moment of his life, David, "a man after [God's] own heart" (Acts 13:22), knew that God was the author of his life and loved him from everlasting to everlasting (Jer. 31:3).

Everyone reading this book has a life story. Yeah, you have a life story. A story that entails the ups and downs, the bitter and sweet, misfortune and fortune, sickness and health, sin and redemption. You have been involved in situations that you know were not right, just or honorable; you ran when you needed to stand, cried when you needed to count it all joy, and rejected God's Word rather than hide it in your heart. You have also done great deeds: You have committed to helping the sick and shut in, offered acts of kindness to others, shared all that God has given to you, answered to the voice of God, prayed for others, and sought to be pleasing unto the Lord.

Whatever your life situation and story, you must always remember that God is aware of every letter, word, comma, space, exclamation point, question mark and period. God exists in every line and moment of your life, whether you acknowledge Him or not. God is God. It is because of God that you exist and have your being. He is your genetic makeup. It's not just DNA and all that other stuff. It's GOD. Can you see God in all the moments and pages of your life? Can you see God today in your life situation? He is your life story, which is put together and maintained by His love, mercy, and grace.

God exists in every line and moment of your life.

Faith Affirmation: *God is everlasting to everlasting in my life.*

Prayer: Lord, I thank You for today (Ps. 118:24). Every day will I bless You and worship Your holy name (Ps. 145:2). You are Jehovah Shammah, the One who is always there (Heb. 13:5). Whatever my life situation and story, I will remember that You exist in every line and moment. It is because of You that I exist and have my being (Acts 17:28). You are God, and You love me from everlasting to everlasting.

Dear God Letter: Talk to God about your day. Remember God exists in every moment of your day. He is the author of **your life story**.

Dear God,

RESUSCITATION AND RESTORATION

♡♡

And [the Lord] said unto [Ezekiel], Son of man, can these bones live? . . . Again, He said unto [Ezekiel], Prophesy unto these bones, and say unto them, O ye dry bones, hear the word of the LORD. . . So [Ezekiel] prophesied. . . and the bones came together. . . and the breath came into them, and they lived, and stood upon their feet, an exceeding great army (Ezek. 37:3-10).

In the valley of dry bones there were people, in fact, a great army, who had been dead for some time, and the only remnants were their dry bones (Ezek. 37:1-14). The dry bones represented the Israelites, the chosen people of God, who were spiritually dead. The Israelites had lost hope in the promises of God, which left them empty and making decisions outside of God's will. God's people had become the walking dead and were vulnerable to deception, defeat, and death. With time, the people repented and God forgave them of their sins and once again revealed His plans for their future.

Today, Christians can also find themselves in the valley of the dry bones. They have turned from God and are experiencing spiritual and emotional death. Some Christians no longer feel the joy of the Lord, which is their strength (Neh. 8:10). Yes, they smile and even laugh at a few jokes, but deep inside they don't feel the freedom of joy. They wonder what happened to their joy. They wonder if it will return. Some Christians have stopped dreaming. They have decided to accept a mediocre life. After all, their dreams have only lead to disappointment. They are not where they had hoped or planned to be in life. They've asked God for a miracle, but He has not answered – in their time–so they stop dreaming and believing. Their life was once filled with an abundance of hope and zeal. Now their life is filled with disappointment, shame, and defeat. They have spent months and/or years in the valley of dry bones. Other Christians find themselves not experiencing God's peace. Their lives are overwhelmed with frustration, worry, and negative thinking. They find themselves in constant confrontations or avoiding situations. They have difficulty concentrating and/or falling asleep at night. They experience constant fear, which has covered their peace and seems to be tormenting them (1 Jn. 4:18). They experience one hopeless thought after another. They can't muster the energy to find rest in God's peace. They spend months and years in the valley of dry bones.

Living in the valley of dry bones is not God's will for our lives. As Christians, we are filled with God, the Holy Spirit and have the power and authority in the name of Jesus to prophesy unto the situation. We have the power to resist Satan in the name of Jesus (Jas. 4:7) and to order our thoughts and emotions to line up with the Word of God. We also have the power and authority to command our life situation to line up with the Word of God, thus saith the Lord; God shall bring forth deliverance and ye shall know that God lives.

Take the time to search your life for dry bones – those remnants that are contributing to your emotional or spiritual death, hidden in your heart, and exposed through your thoughts and actions. Expose your bones to God and command your bones in the name of Jesus to line up with God's Word. Believe that God will restore and resuscitate your life. You must believe and walk knowing that restoration has occurred; "for we walk by faith and not by sight" (2 Cor. 5:7).

Your bones will be restored and renewed because of God's love for you. Ezekiel prophesied to the dry bones as he was commanded by God, and as he prophesied "there was a noise, and behold a shaking, and the bones came together, bone to his bone . . . and the breath came into them, and they lived, and stood up upon their feet, an exceeding great army" (Ezek. 37:7-10). God had put His spirit back into these men, and they lived. Receive God's Word and your bones and spirit shall be renewed. God shall restore you to your rightful place with Him. You shall declare that you are alive because the Lord has quickened your spirit.

Faith Affirmation: *My dry bones have been brought back to life in the name of Jesus Christ.*

Prayer: Lord, this is the day that You have made (Ps. 118:24). You encouraged me and showed me how to open my heart that I would receive more of Your love. It is Your will that I experience the fullness of life. "Thou art my God, and I will praise thee: thou art my God, I will exalt thee" (Ps.

118:28). Father, I ask that You search me, forgive me, and renew a right spirit within me (Ps. 51:10).

Dear God Letter: Talk to God about your day. You must believe and walk knowing your mind, body, and spirit will **be resuscitated and restored** by God in the name of Jesus.

Dear God,

THE WAY OUT

Jesus saith unto him, I am the way, the truth, and the life: no man cometh unto the Father, but by me (Jn. 14:6).

The little boy eyed the wooden banister and then decided to push his head between the poles. Next, he wiggled the rest of his body through the poles and was inside of the enclosed area. He sat a while, played a while and even took a short nap. When he awoke from his nap, he played a little longer and then decided it was time to go home. He pushed his head back through the bars, but it didn't seem as easy as the first time. Upon getting his head through the bars, he began to work his body through, but it just wouldn't go through the bars. Then he tried to pull his head back out. It was difficult, but he managed to get it out; yet he was still stuck. How could this be? It had not been very difficult to squeeze through earlier that day.

The little boy continued to try to get his head and body through the bars for what seemed to be hours, but to no avail. He would need help. He tried to stay calm, but it was getting late, and he was getting scared. He cried out, "I'm stuck. I'm stuck. Somebody help me. I'm stuck," but no one answered or came to his rescue. Would he die in this place? He began to yell again, "Help, Help, I can't get out." After what seemed to be a lifetime, he heard his father's voice. He turned, and his father was right inside of his stuck place. He held his son and told him that everything was going to be alright. He was right there with him and would show him the way out.

Most recently I realized I was stuck. I was stuck in my career. My career has had its ups and downs. I've learned a lot on my way to professional success. I have developed programs, built relationships, and worked really hard – did I say worked really hard. I've grown as a professional, but I feel it's time for me to make a change – move on. Yet, I'm still in the same job and career.

While I was driving home one day, I began to talk to God about my "stuck" situation. He led me to His throne of grace and mercy. I acknowledged that I didn't know how to leave, let alone know where I would go or what I would do. I was stuck. I know a lot of stuff, but I don't know how to get myself unstuck. I don't know how to step out. I needed God's help. I acknowledged with a humble heart that I needed help, help, and help. My heart was humble, and my soul was weeping. I experienced a genuine moment with myself and God.

With all my education and know how, I had gotten myself stuck, and only my Father could get me out. Within the next week, a friend called me about a job opportunity. God gave me three scriptures. You are well able to possess the land (Num. 13:30). I must "trust in the Lord with all [my] heart; and lean not unto my own understanding. In all [my] ways acknowledge Him and He shall direct my paths" (Prov. 3:5-6). I'm still in my job, but my heart and attitude have changed. I am trusting God to deliver me to my next destination. Does any of my testimony sound familiar? If so, seek God and join me and others as we travel with God to our next destination. All aboard!

Faith Affirmation: *God you are my way, truth, and light.*

Prayer: Lord, I thank You for today (Ps. 118:24), another day to experience Your comfort. You are great, and "[Your] greatness is unsearchable" (Ps. 145:3). I must seek You (Matt. 6:33). I will hide Your word in my heart (Ps. 119:11) and keep my heart focused on You (Prov. 4:23). Your way is right, just and perfect for me (Ps. 18:30-32).

Dear God Letter: Talk to God about your day. God will show **you the way out.** He will deliver you to your next destination.

Dear God,

Date:
Day #:

THE PERFECT ONE – GOD

Be ye therefore perfect, even as your Father which is in heaven is perfect (Matt. 5:48).

Some days I just want to be perfect. I don't want to deal with the negativity, challenges, and adversities of life. I don't want to feel sadness, uncertainty, disappointment or fear. I just want to be perfect and live a perfect life. I also want everything I do to be perfect. How about you? Do you sometimes, or most of the time, want to be perfect? It would allow us to tell others what to do instead of them telling us what to do, how to do it, and when to do it. We would have the perfect look, walk, talk, feelings, ideas, thoughts, suggestions, solutions, praise, prayer, and worship. We could do no wrong. We would be happy and joyful all the time.

There is a catch to being perfect. It would give us a lot of power and control, which at some point we would misuse. We would always be all that! Basically, we would be miniature gods, and therefore, we would not need to honor God. Wait a minute (as our Dad would say), there is only One God (Eph. 4:4-6). He is the creator of the world and all that is within it (Ps. 24:1) –that includes us. He alone is God and has sovereign authority and power.

> *God is the only One who is perfect.*

God is the only One who is perfect. He is righteous, holy, and just and so much more. He offers unconditional love. He is not prideful, boastful or judgmental. Praise God, that He created children, not little perfect gods. God created us for His will and purpose (Isa. 43:7). He created us in his own image and likeness (Gen. 1: 26). He knew that if His creations were perfect, they would be prideful, jealous, evil, controlling, abusive, "off the hook," which would cause spiritual death, and they would not inherit the kingdom of God (Eph. 5:5).

287

God did not call us to be perfect in the flesh. He called us to greater works through Him (Jn. 14:12). God called us to become like Him through His love and perfect way. There is not a perfect person, situation, book, business project, husband, wife, child, relationship. However, there is what is right, just, and pleasing unto God. Seek God so that He can take you into His perfect love, peace, joy, and character as you journey with Him on your road to reaching "the prize of the high calling of God in Christ Jesus" (Phil. 3:14).

Faith Affirmation: *Lord, I strive to stand perfect and complete in Your will.*

Prayer: Lord, I thank You for another day to do Your will (Ps. 118:24). I will praise You Lord. Your glory is above the earth and the heavens (Ps. 57:5). You are God, the Perfect One, and "there is no God beside [You]" (Isa. 45:5). "It is [You] that girdeth me with strength, and maketh my way perfect" (Ps. 18:32). I strive to stand perfect and complete in Your will (Col. 4:12).

Dear God Letter: Talk to God about your day. **God, the only perfect One**, lives within you, and you are complete only in Him.

Dear God,

Date:
Day #:

LOADED WITH BENEFITS

Blessed be the Lord, who daily loadeth us with benefits, even the God of our salvation (Ps. 68:19).

G od is. He is I AM THAT I AM (Ex. 3:14). He is God, and He daily loads you with benefits and blessings – more than you can count or even comprehend (Ps. 68:19). He just loads (pours out) a whole bunch of good stuff. He loads you with an infinite number of benefits. The blessings are there in the good and bad times. I heard a woman say that if the Lord stopped blessing her today she would still need to forever praise Him. I can't even fathom the Lord not blessing me. I am His child and can do nothing without Him. I need Him each and every day.

At the end of one day, I tried to count my benefits and blessings. I thought–He woke me up. I took a morning stretch. I'm breathing. I can walk and talk. I can hear. I can think, feel and taste. God loves me. My family loves me. My husband loves me. I have beautiful children. The sky is blue. The leaves on the trees are beautiful. God sent His only begotten Son for me. My children's laughter brings forth my laughter. Life seems pretty stressful right now but God's already gone before me today to make the crooked places straight (Isa. 45:2). I can rest assured that God's plan for my life includes peace and prosperity (Jer. 29:11). I saw a beautiful sunset. I talked with my sisters this morning. I laughed. I called a friend. God charged His angels to watch over me and to keep me in all my ways (Ps. 91:11). I smiled over and over again and it brought warmth to my soul. My heart was pounding. My blood was working through my body and keeping me warm and alive. God chose to give me life.

At some point, I paused and stopped counting. What was I thinking? That I could count all of my benefits? I was not close to counting all of them. I ended with God loves me, which is where I should have begun. I thanked God for daily loading me with His benefits, those seen and unseen.

We often take so much for granted. We assume that life is just a given; but, it's not. We have a life because of God's unconditional love. No matter the situation or circumstance, God still loads you with benefits. Take the time today no matter how you are feeling or what you're experiencing to acknowledge God's infinite love and benefits. Take the time to scan your day and thank God for all He has done for you.

Faith Affirmation: *God loads me with His benefits every day.*

Prayer: Lord, I thank You for today (Ps. 118:24). You are great and "greatly to be praised" (Ps. 145:3). "Blessed be the Lord, who daily loadeth [me] with benefits" (Ps. 68:19) and blessings. Lord, open my heart that I may receive Your love. I ask that You open my eyes that I may see my daily benefits. Open my spirit that I may truly be thankful for Your daily benefits. Open my mouth and heart that I might share my testimony of Your love.

Dear God Letter: Talk to God about your day. **God daily loads you with His benefits**.

Dear God,

BOUGHT AND KEPT

For ye are bought with a price: therefore glorify God in your body, and in your spirit, which are God's (1 Cor. 6:20).

In 1968, Shirley Chisholm became the first Black American woman elected to Congress. In 1972, she became the first Black American female to seek a major party's presidential nomination in the United States. She paved the trail for Barack Obama to become the first Black American president of the United States. Additionally, she paved the way for Hilary Clinton to become the first female to accept the nominee of the Democratic Party for President of the United States.

Chisholm was a strong woman who fought for change and created change. Her campaign slogan and first book were titled *Unbought and Unbossed*. When she was asked how she wanted to be remembered, Shirley Chisholm replied, "When I die, I want to be remembered as a woman who lived in the 20th century and who dared to be a catalyst of change. . . I want to be remembered as a woman who fought for change in the 20th century. That's what I want." Chisholm died on New Year's Day 2005, a day in the United States that recognizes new beginnings, commitments, and change; how appropriate.

I began to think about how I wanted to be remembered. My life's slogan shall be "Bought and Kept," I am a child of the Most High God. I have been bought with a price, the crucifixion and resurrection of Jesus Christ (1 Pet. 1:18-19; 1 Cor. 6:19-20). I have been kept by God, the Good Shepherd (Jn. 10:11, 14), the Bread of Life (Jn. 6:35), The Way, the Truth, and the Life (Jn. 14:6), the True Vine (Jn. 15:1), the Resurrection and the Life (Jn. 11:25). I have been kept by I AM THAT I AM (Ex. 3:14). My body is the temple of God and the Holy Spirit dwells within me (1 Cor. 3:16).

I am called in the name of Jesus Christ to be many things: a friend to the friendless; a shelter to the homeless; a comfort to the sick; God's hope in the face of despair; a warrior in the name of Jesus; and a voice declaring the Good News of Jesus Christ (Mk. 16:15). I am also called to stand in the gap for those in need; love my neighbors; stand with my shield of faith (Eph. 6:16); pray unceasingly (1 Thess. 5:17); give thanks (1 Thess. 5:18); and rejoice for evermore (1 Thess. 5:16) in the name of Jesus.

I acknowledge that I have been bought with the blood of Jesus and kept by the Holy Spirit and God's unconditional love. I want people to know that I have been "Bought and Kept" in the name of Jesus. I also want my life to reflect the love and power of Jesus Christ. This is my life's slogan "Bought and Kept." What's your life's slogan?

Faith Affirmation: *(Your Life's Slogan)* _____

_____
_____
_____
_____.

Prayer: Lord, I thank You for this day (Ps. 118:4). I thank You for loving me. "For thou art great, and doest wondrous things: thou art God alone" (Ps. 86:10). I have been bought with the blood of Your son, Jesus Christ (1 Cor. 6:20, Jn. 3:16). I am Your child, and I will share the good news of Jesus Christ. My life's slogan shall be that I have been "Bought and Kept" by the Most High God, and I shall always serve Him. I love You, Lord.

Dear God Letter: Talk to God about your day. Remember you were **bought with a price, the crucifixion of Jesus Christ and kept by God's unconditional love.**

Dear God,

Date:
Day #:

A Child's Voice
WHERE I'M FROM

But now, O LORD, thou art our Father; we are the clay, and thou our potter; and we all are the work of your hand (Isa. 64:8).

I am from Thumper, from soul food, and singing in the shower.
I am from the aroma of flowers in the morning to the sweet plums on our plum tree with its long arms that wave to you in the wind.
I am from cooking on Christmas and celebrating the birth of Christ;
From my dad's love of math and talkin' loud, to my mom's love of writing and helping others.

I am from a family that's always talking to a family that's always cleaning.
From stop that and put that down!
I am from read the Bible and hurry up so we can get to church on time.
I am from Seattle, rainin' day and night, to the sweltering heat in Alabama, Oklahoma, and Louisiana.

I am from albums filled with now and then. From what's that and I remember.
From the grandparents who prayed for their children and shared their love to the family that cared for everyone.

I am from Slavery and Freedom, from Sojourner Truth, and Harriet Tubman, to the Civil Rights Movement, to Dr. Martin Luther King Jr.'s dream, Rosa Park's stand for equality, Malcolm X's fight for justice and President Obama's "Yes, We Can!

Most of all, I am from God and a family that loves me!
That's where I'm from –
Where are you from?

Faith Affirmation: *I am from God, my Lord and Savior.*

Prayer: Lord, I thank You for this day (Ps. 118:24). I shall praise and worship Your holy name forever. You formed me in my mother's womb and created me in Your likeness and image (Gen. 1:26). You breathed Your spirit of life into me and called me to fulfill my divine purpose. You filled me with You, the Holy Spirit (1 Cor. 3:16), and promised to guide and direct my path (Prov. 3:5-6). I have had many life experiences, but through them all, You have watched over me and loved me. It's an honor and privilege to say that I am Your child. I love You!

Dear God Letter: Talk to God about your day. **You come from God,** and you were created to praise and worship Him and to do His will.

Dear God,

Date:

Day #:

DEAR GOD, I LOVE YOU

I will love thee, *O LORD, my strength (Ps. 18:1)*.

D ear God,
I Love You.
I Love You, You, You.
I think about You all the time.
I felt Your peace this morning, and I thought about You.
I felt Your joy today, and I thought about You.
I smiled with the dawning of the morning, and I thought about You.
I felt love today, and I thought about You.
I felt the warmth of the sun today, and I thought about You.
I watched the quiet breeze cause the tree leaves to sway and wave today,
and I thought about You.
I thought how excellent and wonderful You are.
I thought how righteous and holy You are.
I thought how great thou art.
I thought You love –me.

I felt Your presence today, and I thought about You.
I faced temptation today, and I thought about You.
I thought to make the right choice in the name of Jesus.
It is my desire to please You.

I made mistakes today, and I thought about You.
I thought that You continue to love me even though I am not perfect.
You love me even though You know the secrets of my heart and my deepest
thoughts.

I cried today, and I thought about You.
I thanked You for washing away my tears and comforting my heart.

295

I showed compassion today, and I thought about You
I thanked and praised You for filling my heart with love.

Lord, I love You, You, You.
I will continue to think about You all the time.
Thinking about You brings a smile to my face;
Laughter to my heart; and peace and joy to my soul.
When I think about You, I feel Your joy, love, peace, and power.
When I think about You, once again all things become possible through You.
I Love You, You, You.
I will love You always and forever and ever and ever . . . !

Faith Affirmation: *I love the Lord.*

Prayer: Lord, I praise Your name. You are amazing, awesome and excellent, and Your love endures forever (Ps. 118:4). I thank You for loving me so much that You provided me with another day to tell You how much I love You. I think about You all the time, and I want You to know how much I love You. I love You more than words can express. I love You, and I will love You always and forever!

Dear God Letter: Talk to God about your day. Remember to tell **God that you will love Him always and forever.**

Dear God,

AUTHORS' NOTE

We pray that this book and your 101-days walk has been a blessing to you and others. We pray that your walk with God will continue, and you will see Him to behold the beauty of the Lord. We encourage you to continue pressing toward the mark of the prize of the Most High calling. We also encourage you to stay faithful and committed to your calling and God. Let your hope always be in the Lord.

We recommend that you take the time to reflect on your 101-days walk with God and talk to God about it. He loves you and has so much in store for you. His love is always and forever. We also recommend that within 30, 60 or 90 days you assess your walk with God and commit to a 10, 15, 20, or 30 days walk with Him. During this time, you can again talk with Him about your current situation and life long journey with Him. You may want to commit to a certain number of days of praise, worship, positive comments and actions, sharing God's word with others or other actions that will build you up and enhance your walk with God. Just keep on keeping on your **Intentional Walk with God.**

ABOUT THE AUTHORS

Yvonne L. Terrell-Powell is a Spirit filled woman of God. She is the founder of Speak Life. Speak Life is a ministry dedicated to reminding individuals that God loves them, and encouraging and inspiring them to live a Christ filled life. Speak Life offers seminars, workshops, conferences, coaching, and personal counseling based on the Word of God. Yvonne is a licensed mental health counselor, skilled facilitator, and dynamic presenter and teacher. She received her doctoral degree from the Pennsylvania State University in Counseling Psychology. Yvonne is married, and she has two children. She resides in Seattle, Washington with her family.

Jenel A. Terrell-Matias is a Spirit filled woman of God and an intercessor. She is the co-founder of Speak Life. Jenel established the Wailing Wall of Ebenezer, a wall for believers to bring their prayers. She ministers to women who are incarcerated. Jenel is also a skilled facilitator and dynamic teacher. She received her Bachelor of Arts degree from National University in Behavioral Science. Jenel resides in Vacaville, California with her husband and daughter. She has six children, and she is the proud grandparent of eleven grandchildren.

References

What Do You See?
1. Martin, Bill Jr. (1970). Brown bear, brown bear, what do you see? New York: NY: Henry Holt and Co.

He's Closer Than You Think
1. Houghton, I. (2011). Jesus at the center. Integrity Worship Music.

Is There Not A Cause?
1. Sojourner Truth speeches and commentary. http://www.sojournertruth.org/Library/Speeches/.
2. Pao, M. (2016). Cesar Chavez http://www.npr.org/2016/08/02/488428577/cesar-chavez-the-life-behind-a-legacy-of-farm-labor-rightsvez: the life behind legacy of farm labor rights. NPR.
3. Mother Teresa. Wikipedia. https://en.wikipedia.org/wiki/Mother_Teresa
4. Biography.com Editors (2015). Mahatma Gandhi biography. The Biography.com website. http://www.biography.com/people/mahatma-gandhi-9305898.

Pressing
1. Tombstone (1993). Hollywood Pictures. http://www.tcm.com/tcmdb/title/18835/Tombstone/.

The Names Of God Have Power
1. Spangler, A. (2010). Journal: Praying the names of God. TN: Ellie Claire, Worthy Publishing.
2. Evans, T. (2016). Praying and pronouncing the names of God. As spoken by Tony Evans http://tonyevans.org/praying-and-pronouncing-the-names-of-god/.

Faith In God Testimonies
1. Alzheimer Association (2016). http://www.alz.org/.

This Is Your Life
1. This is your life. https://en.wikipedia.org/wiki/This_Is_Your_Life

Sweet Epiphany
1. Wade, J. F. (1751). O come, all ye faithful (Adeste fideles).

Naked I Came
1. The Sugar Hill Gang (1979). Rappers delight.
2. The Chi-lites (1971). Have you seen her. Brunswick Records.
3. Silbar, J. & Henley, L. (1982). Wind beneath my wings.
4. McClurkin, D. (2011). Great is your mercies toward me.
5. Klein, L. (1992). I love you, Lord.
6. Franklin, A (1972). What a friend we have in Jesus. Atlantic Records.
7. Van DeVenter, J. W. (1896). I surrender all.

A Strange Thing Happened On The Way To A Blessing
1. Vaughn, T. (2007). A strange thing happened on the way to a blessing. Sermon delivered by Thomazine Vaughn at Righteous Fellowship. Written interpretation of sermon by Yvonne Terrell-Powell (2007).

Bought And Kept
1. Chisholm, S. (1970). Unbought and unbossed. Boston: Houghton Mifflin.
2. Lynch, S. (2005). Remembering Shirley Chisholm. Washington Post. http://www.washingtonpost.com/wp-dyn/articles/A44343-2005Jan3.html.

A Child's Voice: Where I'm From
1. Powell, U. (2006). A child's voice: Where I'm from. Unpublished poem.

CPSIA information can be obtained
at www.ICGtesting.com
Printed in the USA
LVHW040735291020
669936LV00002B/149